Fiction in the Field

Fiction in the Field

Creative Writing Across Disciplines

Jacqueline Yallop

BLOOMSBURY ACADEMIC
LONDON · NEW YORK · OXFORD · NEW DELHI · SYDNEY

BLOOMSBURY ACADEMIC
Bloomsbury Publishing Plc, 50 Bedford Square, London, WC1B 3DP, UK
Bloomsbury Publishing Inc, 1359 Broadway, New York, NY 10018, USA
Bloomsbury Publishing Ireland, 29 Earlsfort Terrace, Dublin 2, D02 AY28, Ireland

BLOOMSBURY, BLOOMSBURY ACADEMIC and the Diana logo
are trademarks of Bloomsbury Publishing Plc

First published in Great Britain 2026

Copyright © Jacqueline Yallop, 2026

Jacqueline Yallop has asserted her right under the Copyright, Designs and Patents Act, 1988, to be identified as Author of this work.

For legal purposes the Acknowledgements on p. vi constitute
an extension of this copyright page.

Cover design and illustration © Gita Govinda Kowlessur

All rights reserved. No part of this publication may be: i) reproduced or transmitted in any form, electronic or mechanical, including photocopying, recording or by means of any information storage or retrieval system without prior permission in writing from the publishers; or ii) used or reproduced in any way for the training, development or operation of artificial intelligence (AI) technologies, including generative AI technologies. The rights holders expressly reserve this publication from the text and data mining exception as per Article 4(3) of the Digital Single Market Directive (EU) 2019/790.

Bloomsbury Publishing Plc does not have any control over, or responsibility for, any third-party websites referred to or in this book. All internet addresses given in this book were correct at the time of going to press. The author and publisher regret any inconvenience caused if addresses have changed or sites have ceased to exist, but can accept no responsibility for any such changes.

A catalogue record for this book is available from the British Library.
A catalog record for this book is available from the Library of Congress.

ISBN: HB: 978-1-3504-4467-6
       PB: 978-1-3504-4468-3
       ePDF: 978-1-3504-4469-0
       eBook: 978-1-3504-4470-6

Typeset by Integra Software Serivces Pvt. Ltd.
Printed and bound in Great Britain

For product safety related questions contact productsafety@bloomsbury.com.

To find out more about our authors and books visit www.bloomsbury.com
and sign up for our newsletters.

Contents

Acknowledgements vi

Introduction 1

1. Narrative Time/Archaeology 9
2. Character/Genetics 35
3. Narrative Structure/Architecture 61
4. Plot/Medicine 83
5. Point of View/Law 105
6. Worldbuilding/Botanical Science 131

Three Words 151

Notes 155
Selected Bibliography 168
Index 171

Acknowledgements

Sincere thanks are due to everyone who agreed to talk to me for this book. The conversations we had were, without exception, provocative, inspiring and thoroughly entertaining. So, thanks to Tim Murray, Ian Armit, Rosemary Joyce, Misha Angrist, Kevin Mitchell, Brigitte Nerlich, Pedro Gadanho, Matteo Pericoli, Gordon Grice, Nellie Hermann, Steven Hastings, John Launer, Supardi Supardi, Keith Belzer, Jeanine Skorinko, Nirupa Rao, Octavia Cade, and Jen Sloane for so generously sharing their expertise, taking my questions seriously and making time for discussion. I've attempted to be completely faithful in my transcription of these conversations and their subsequent interpretation. If any errors have crepot in, I apologize. Thanks, too, to my brilliant colleagues in the Department of English and Creative Writing at Aberystwyth University who listened to these chapters in development during research seminars and who responded with invaluable and positive suggestions for improvement. I am also very grateful to the University for the award of a significant period of research leave, which enabled me to give this project the attention it deserves.

Introduction

Why do we write? One reason might be: to better understand the world. To get a grip on what it means to be here, now, a part of this thing that is being alive. But writers are no more alone in this pursuit of knowledge about the human condition than they are in spending hours at a keyboard. The drive to make sense of, and express, human experience is the heart beating at the core of the arts and humanities more generally – and the same heartbeat pulsing in all kinds of disciplines beyond. Why do we write? To understand. Why do scientists, doctors, lawyers, engineers practice? To understand, too. This mutual purpose is offered then as the obvious starting point for a project that marries key creative writing techniques with processes and approaches in a range of other disciplines, with the aim of discovering shared practice.

This project is primarily about process. It concerns itself less with outputs – with the finished product of a novel or an experiment; a short story or a medical diagnosis – than with methods of conceptualization. How do we think and work as writers of fiction? How do experts in other disciplines construct their methodologies? Are there points at which these practices collide? As with all research projects, there is the inevitable influence of my own interests and inherent biases, but by organizing this inquiry around conversations with professionals in other fields, I've hoped to contain and mitigate these. My investigation has been driven by dialogues with extraordinary specialists in a range of subjects, all of whom have brought new perspectives to the task. I have attempted to make these conversations as diverse as possible, and to ensure that they challenge, rather than simply reinforce, my thinking. I have tried to engage in open-ended conversations that are guided by the expertise of my contributor rather than proscribed by my preconceptions and pre-prepared questions. Nonetheless, these conversations are not (and could never be) exhaustive. There are those who declined to speak to me and those I never sought out or who could not, in the end, find the time to talk; there are the vast number of specialists with inspirational ideas who never even made it to the Teams calendar. This had to be a finite project. I've had to make choices about my interlocutors. As a result, the direction of the research has inevitably been determined by the views and priorities of those I've been speaking to; there are biases here, too, and gaps, loose ends and detours. But for all these shortcomings, the meetings that have enabled this book have been wide-ranging and energizing, offering a series of conceptual, textual, spatial, creative and material intersections that have made explicit what are often implicit modes of thinking. They have been excellent conversations, and this is my attempt to write about them.

In 1858, the German historian, Johann Droysen, proposed three scientific methods which he identified as the speculative, the mathematical or physical, and the historical, each characterized by a distinct impulse, which he identified respectively as to know (*wissen*), to explain (*erklären*) and to understand (*verstehen*). Droyen's separation of these methodologies, dissociating speculation from understanding, for example, is often read as a crucial moment not only in formulating an approach to history, but more broadly in splitting what we now recognize as the humanities from the sciences, establishing autonomous realms of knowledge which subsequently appeared to head off in different directions. This nineteenth-century split between the humanities and the sciences – and particularly between imaginative practice and knowledge-based methodology – also signalled a fracture in ways of thinking about narrative and story, where these elements might belong, and how they might accrue validity and status as research tools. The application of the imagination as a way of understanding and explaining, equal to but distinct from evidence, for example, became increasingly suspect, and is still regarded as dubious in many academic and professional contexts. The textual expression of the imaginative act in a work of fiction was regarded as naturally and rightly separate to the evidencing of the more scientific act in such things as the research paper, the archaeological dig or the architectural construct. More recently, the educational separation of creative practice and STEM subjects remains firmly embedded in schools and universities, despite the best efforts of interdisciplinary practitioners, ensuring that Droysen's ways of knowing, explaining and understanding tend still to be regarded as divergent. It should be noted here, too, that the resistance is not entirely one sided: fiction writing is often regarded as a self-contained bubble of creative practice, with teaching and analysis content to focus on craft and genre, without reference to other disciplinary fields.

With the uncoupling of research fields along Droysensian lines, the notion of fiction as a driver of either scientific discovery or the day-to-day delivery of cutting-edge investigation has become something of an oddity. There is broad acceptance of the truism that, as humans, we instinctively employ story to make sense of the world. It's been shown that we construct our memories and our life stories in a similar way to the writing of fiction, creating time frames, characters and themes, embedding plots and suspense. Our stories change as time passes as well as in different contexts and company; we reshape them constantly through conversations and interactions, presenting and re-presenting narratives that fit the occasion. But while story might be firmly lodged in our sense of self, the idea that it can be an active mode of serious investigation has gained less credence. The work of story/fiction does not easily conform to scientific methodologies; ultimately it only allows interpretation and resists explanation. In addition, the imaginative act of writing demands another in the act of reading; results can (should?) be unsettling, unpredictable and contested.

Some of the disciplines discussed in this book have traditions of working across the arts, humanities and sciences, and naturally straddle methodologies and approaches. In so doing, they have ventured a sometimes tentative engagement with narrative in general and story in particular. As a 'soft science', archaeology often embraces the imaginative act of reconstruction, for example, alongside the data evidence of the material record. The practice of law, as a social science, engages with notions of histories and texts that are the bedrock of humanities. For many years, architects have been debating what a narrative approach might mean for their practice and how (or if) a building might be said to tell a story. The recognition that shared principles of story *do* often bring together different disciplines is firmly established. As Roland Barthes has pointed out, the act of creating a narrative requires the convergence of 'a prodigious variety of genres', enabling different fields to imagine, theorize and borrow from each other.[1] It's this first point of contact that sparks the conversations recounted here. But it's also with a certain wariness that I've begun to piece together 'a prodigious variety' of discussions about what fiction is and how it might be embedded in other professions. Despite many disciplines dipping into narrative theory and practice, as outlined in the examples above and more thoroughly in the chapters that follow, the validity of fictional approaches and the influence of storytelling structure have also been openly opposed: in archaeology, for example, questions around the use of story as an interpretive tool have been fiercely debated over several decades with many rejecting any act of fictionalization. While many professionals from all walks of life now (perhaps grudgingly) accept that shared processes can be valuable and can offer new insights, the notion of accepting story as one of these key processes can still be a step too far. Although it's broadly acknowledged that most disciplines work with some form of distinctive narrative, with its implications of formality and cool restraint, the idea that they may make use of fiction or story – bound to the less controllable forces of the imaginative act – tends to be much less acceptable.

We will explore distinctions between narrative and story briefly below and at more length in the body of the book. Here I simply want to place a marker: this inquiry starts from the conviction that not only narrative but explicitly the fictionalization of experience has a fundamental role to play beyond the pages of a novel. But it's important to be clear that I'm not trying to suggest that fiction and its processes somehow accrue value by being partnered with, or viewed adjacent to, other activity, or that creative practice requires a connection to a STEM subject, for example, to become meaningful. Writing (and reading) does not need to 'engage' with anything beyond itself to be relevant and eloquent. It is an important and influential activity in its own right. Nor is this project about allowing fiction and its techniques to comment on what might be regarded as the more serious business being conducted by grown-ups, like some kind of querulous child brought along to the office on work experience. As writers, there are always things we can learn from all manner of sources; we're always in search of new challenges. But this conversation does not lead in one direction. Writers have skills, techniques and approaches they can lend to other disciplines; there is expertise we can share. So what drives this project is a belief in mutuality. In the same way that fiction might be informed or shaped by a new appreciation of other fields of knowledge, so other professions can profit from understanding more about what we do as writers and how this impacts on their work. It's in this spirit that each chapter includes short cross-disciplinary exercises and discussion points, volunteered as a means of testing some of the ideas in a practical way.

Fiction in the Field, as the title suggests, is concerned with the craft of the writer specific to fiction, in both the short story and the novel. Other creative writing genres – poetry, scripts for radio, television and film, gaming narratives, memoir – require particular skills, and in the hope of containing an already broad discourse, the specific focus on fiction techniques allows, I hope, some clarity of direction. Similarly, the book is primarily concerned, as noted above, with process rather than product, which inevitably means that some interesting intersections have had to be laid aside: I don't discuss historical fiction written by archaeologists and developed from their professional practice, for example, or the dramatization of courtroom events for the public. Since my concern is with the possibilities of fictional narrative as a new point of knowledge, I also work across genres, taking prompts from my interlocutors' reading or critical debate; in this way the connections between genetics and speculative fiction came to the fore, while discussions about the handling of narrative time are illustrated with analyses of realist examples. Where possible, I've tried to make clear within each chapter's discussion how choices have been made and why particular directions have been followed.

While the conversations that structure this book, and my reflections on them, necessarily touch on narrative theory, this again is intentionally restricted to a modest sub-plot, recognizing that it presents an extensive line of inquiry in its own right, which is thoroughly rehearsed elsewhere and which would require more attention than I'm able to give it here. Narratology can be a useful tool, allowing us to better explore the components that make up narrative structure, what meanings they accrue and how they exert an effect on the reader. More widely, it also allows for analysis of the wider implications of any narrative discourse, such as subjectivity, body, race and culture. With this in mind, my approach unavoidably engages with debate about the nature, scope and reach of narrative in a range of disciplines, and the analysis of fiction and story is necessarily informed by the wider context provided by narrative theory. Where possible, however, I've tried to acknowledge these resonances, without dwelling on them. While I pause momentarily on key theorists and their work, citing Ricœur on narrative time and Bakhtin's concept of the chronotope for example, this is only where it feels necessary for a clear understanding of the discussion to follow. In Chapter 1, I also briefly address definitions of story in theoretical terms, distinguishing it from discourse; in my analysis of narrative medicine in Chapter 4, I consider ways in which we define and understand plot. But since this is a book about fiction as practice, and about the creative imaginative act in particular, I use terms such as 'story', 'narrative' and 'plot' in what theorists might consider a loose fashion at times. In a personal and discursive exploration, my intention has been to maintain an emphasis on writing as doing rather than as text.

Perhaps the most significant influence of narrative theory here is in the choice of creative writing techniques on which the book is predicated and which form the basis for each chapter: narrative time, character, structure, plot, point of view and worldbuilding. Influential twentieth-century texts, such as Shlomith Rimmon-Kenan's *Narrative Fiction*, Seymour Chatman's *Story and Discourse* and Gérard Genette's *Narrative Discourse*, published in a dynamic period of critical debate between 1978 and 1983, identified central features of narrative that have largely been endorsed by more contemporary theorists. This consensus posits, in general terms, a process of narrative whereby an event occurs within a temporal sequence and specified setting; it happens to, and is caused by, characters or agents, the opening state being subject to change as the narrative progresses in the form of a plot; it's represented for the reader by a speaker who absorbs and reports the event from a particular point of view.

With these simple distilled components of time, characters, narrator, plot and place, all kinds of stories are built, recounted and received.

For the purposes of this book, and as the starting point for each chapter, I have largely borrowed from Georg Lukács a deceptively straightforward sense of narrative as a way of knowing. It's this search for a way of knowing that underpins all the conversations, exchanges and digressions, but such a quest is, of course, enormous. With only a chapter in which to consider each of the different disciplines I encounter – archaeology, genetics, architecture, medicine, law and botanical science – the exploration is inevitably curtailed. Interesting avenues are left unvisited, fascinating facts stay concealed, knowledge remains scant. I have had to make choices about the tiny area of other professions on which to focus attention while recognizing that the discussion can never be exhaustive or representative. I base my investigation of point of view on the Common Law system used in the UK and the United States, for example, rather than attempting to address a different legal tradition; my encounter with current genetics research focuses attention on a relative backwater in its examination of character while turning away from the ocean tides of medical development. Each discipline's interaction with fiction has the potential to fill an entire volume. For the purposes of this book, I have followed what appear to be the most fruitful directions to offer a way into a fascinating but vast subject.

I am not a specialist in anything other than fiction, so my venture into other fields has been as an outsider, a wary tourist on safari. As such, I am fully aware that I have often missed the nuances of scholarship in other disciplines; I've been forced to simplify arguments and curtail debates. I am still learning. This project was not intended to try to assimilate any other distinct discipline, however. The intention is to enter into a genuinely two-way conversation that illuminates both. Within the constraints of this undertaking, my best aim is to raise questions, to tender possibilities and to spark ideas, to highlight the points at which the practice of fiction and the practice of other disciplines seem to speak to each other, and to accent where tensions remain or even where difference might be irreconcilable. I am fully aware that many of the issues discussed here linger unresolved, among them: how does an appreciation of fictional technique achieve the objectives of the other discipline? How do you hold the act of imagination or creativity to account? What practical difference does it make if we recognize mutual ways of thinking? I have attempted to propose some responses to some of these questions, but these remain partial and suggestive. Fortunately, my priority is not so much resolution as embarkation. With the discussions in this book, I'm giving creative writing the chance to venture into the field and prove itself.

1
Narrative Time/ Archaeology

When I was seventeen years old, I came across a small advert at the end of the jobs section in the daily newspaper. No more than four lines long, it simply said that archaeologists were required urgently for a dig in Scotland. I rang the number. Several days later, I was waiting outside Glasgow railway station at six in the morning to catch a minibus that would take me on the winding empty roads to Oban from where we caught the ferry to Stornoway, on the Isle of Lewis in the Outer Hebrides. By evening we were lighting a turf fire in an old farmhouse adjacent to the ancient stone circle at Callanish. For a few weeks at least, I was to be an archaeologist (of sorts).

The farmhouse crouched in the shelter of rocky fields that petered out into a weedy shore of sheep and upturned boats. Wind swept the sky flat. To my eyes, this was an isolated place at the edge of things, but each day we tested this edge, rattling even further west along narrow roads to the excavation site that was tucked in low dunes behind the exposed shore at Cnip, a tiny settlement of a few houses and crofts. Here, a barrage of winter storms had caused sudden and significant erosion revealing a well-preserved Iron-Age wheelhouse complex. Another battering from a ripping Atlantic gale, and it was likely that these ruins would collapse through the sand into the sea. The expedition, of which I was now a part, was the second of two digs by the University of Edinburgh intended to elicit as much information and evidence as possible before the remains were lost.

On Lewis in May, the days are long; they move leisurely towards a late sunset. On site, our hours were long, too, and quiet. Each of us was working in our own way on our own patch; we spoke little. The tide rose and fell within yards of us, but I never saw a walker; few cars past; the handful of residents carefully ignored our intrusion. The weeks were marked only by the austere serenity of island Sundays. And in this kind of suspended existence, absolutely focused on the isolated wheelhouse, I began to learn something about time: I began to discover that it didn't move the way I'd always assumed it did. It wasn't the steady linear progression I believed it to be from childhood observations, a taut wire from which events dangled like pegs on a clothesline. Instead, I began to realize, time could seem more like a strand of sheep wool flapping loosely in the Scottish wind; it bucked and leapt, circled, spun, stretched and contracted; it was present and distant, real and imagined. Sitting in a shallow archaeological trench with the stones of long-ago lives pressed into my jeans, I was no longer millennia away from the first time of this place. The feeling was more like inhabiting a timeline adjacent to the homes here as they had once been, my careful unearthing of drains and firepits not so much a going back as a circling round, a joining up, echoing the observation of the French philosopher and anthropologist, Bruno Latour, that our encounters with time might be more akin to meeting a spiral than a line: 'elements that appear remote if we follow the spiral may turn out to be quite nearby'.[1]

This experience has always suggested to me that there are interesting interactions between how we conceive of and use time in fiction, and how archaeologists engage with time in their work. And at a basic level, the connections seem clear: both practices are intensely focused on ways of moving through and understanding the past in relation to the present, on what the past means, on its legacies and influences; both share a commitment to constructing an intelligent, apparently authentic timeline; both juggle the complex and often contradictory demands inherent in ushering time into a form we might understand. But I'd like to test the hypothesis by considering both the correspondences and contradictions in more detail, so in this chapter I'm speaking to archaeologists to get a more sophisticated understanding of the role time plays in their work and how this might connect with my practice as a writer. In particular, I'm interested in how archaeologists use chronologies to create sequentially ordered stories as a means of interpreting a site, and how far elements of fictionalization might be employed during this process of understanding material evidence.

Written narratives and the influence of the text are deeply embedded in archaeological practice, evolving with – and shaping – the discipline's shift from gentleman's pursuit to science to theoretical study. The field has been constantly rewritten, pieced together from fragments of both the material and textual past. The eighteenth-century stock-in-trade of personal letters to learned societies, frequently couched in flowery, poetic and literary language, was edged out in the nineteenth century by more professional site reports. These tended to offer objective analysis, often with the aim of aligning with emerging scientific narratives (as well as geopolitical conditions), establishing authoritative typologies and distancing the discipline from the 'softer' influences and language of antiquarianism and folklore. Refining this dialogue by the mid-twentieth century, the emphasis was on scholarly papers often expressed in technical terms and proposing hypotheses of the past that could be scientifically tested, with the goal of establishing objective 'laws' by which the past could be read. As in many other disciplines, theories of linguistics and formal literary analysis also made an impact. With the influence of Structuralism in the 1960s, for example, the terms 'reading' and 'writing' became used as a way of engaging not only with literary texts but also with landscapes and objects, forcing archaeologists to reconsider the relationship between the physical reality of a site, the finds it revealed and the language used to discuss and interpret them. Words, texts, the act of writing – the process of constructing narratives – became, for some practitioners at least, integral to ways of thinking about archaeological science.

The work of French theorists such as Saussure, Foucault, Barthes and Derrida, continued to press the link between language and object, increasingly recognizing the complexity of this relationship and showing that for both written texts and archaeological finds, meaning could be indeterminate. As these debates progressed, discussion centered for many archaeologists on the appropriateness of treating an object or a social interaction – a shard of pottery or a burial rite, for example – as a text. Some questioned how far interpretations that relied on the construction of narrative and common to the humanities and disciplines like philosophy and anthropology could be applied to archaeology. This question as to whether assumptions and methods inherent to the narrative process were out of place in an evidence-based science was largely resolved by the turn of the century, however, with a tacit agreement that, in fact, some kind of narrative-building was unavoidable. A more pressing question became what the nature of such a narrative might be, with debate foregrounding the multiplicity of a text and recognizing the transient nature of interpretation, the inevitable presence of the person writing and the values often implicit in addressing evidence. The challenges raised by this debate have, perhaps inevitably, unearthed issues of direct relevance to the fiction writer: the British anthropologist and archaeologist, Barbara Bender, for example, has concluded that 'all accounts, no matter how seemingly factual, how dryly presented, are, in reality, a sort of narrative, a sort of story'.[2] While some in the discipline have made the case for maintaining a clear border between evidence and 'speculation', others have fully embraced this notion of story, suggesting that the transformation of information and knowledge which takes place on examination of material traces and the data they provide is 'a fundamentally creative process', and noting that the distinctions between fact and fiction can sometimes be blurred.[3]

It is this potentially porous border separating fact and fiction that I'm keen to explore, hoping that archaeology's unique position straddling natural and human science – sitting between the 'hard science' of data analysis and the 'persuasive fictions' of ethnography – will enable me to find a crossing point.[4] I recognize that the case for the role of imagination in archaeology, and specifically the recognition of shared fictive techniques, is contentious, but I'm curious to see whether my hypothesis holds up in the face of (or despite) the scepticism of hard science methodologies; I'm heartened, too, by the influence of a softer science approach, which allows for ambiguities and uncertainties. While this softer approach has seen some integration of archaeological interpretation with non-scientific interventions, such as storytelling, poetry and theatre as well as significant discussion about the presence of archaeology in historical fiction, this is not my focus here. Some archaeologists expressly experiment with constructing fictional narrative around gaps in evidence as a research methodology, a process the archaeologist and historical novelist, Victoria Thompson, claims 'allows the multivocality of [the] complex past to assert itself'.[5] In this case, the writing of a fictional account of an event or site is adopted as an analytical tool, with the potential to offer new perspectives on data and material evidence, and test existing hypotheses. The aim is often to provoke an emotional – rather than a scientific – response to the archaeology, with the attention fixed firmly on the role of human agency in constructing the past. Borrowing from the well-worn creative writing adage to show rather than tell, the emphasis is on re/imagined lived experience that 'participates in, contests, augments, and anticipates the stories created by archaeologists'.[6] Some archaeological texts, for example, include consciously fictional vignettes – usually alongside illustrations – which aim to access meaning that might be concealed or obscured by the data, and to humanize and contextualize the evidence provided elsewhere. This approach raises interesting questions about the dangers of anachronism, the difficulties of imagining an irrecoverable past and the inherent problems of empathy, all of which are perhaps particularly relevant to the writer of historical fiction but which I don't have the capacity to explore here. My interest is specifically in the ways in which archaeology approaches notions of time – both in the field and in subsequent analysis – and how this collides with how we use time as writers of fiction.

Time is experienced in most fiction as a series of presences and absences: moments, scenes, events offered to the reader in immersive detail, while other periods of a character's life are completely overlooked or withheld. The writer confronts the demands of a particular incident – a murder, for example, or an arrival – but refuses other incidents considered to be unnecessary, too ordinary or of no significance to the story. Ejected from the time frame of the fiction, these events may sometimes be implied but are generally invisible, even though a reader might assume they have occurred, or even imagine their occurrence without the writer's help: the murderer's hurried breakfast, perhaps, or filling up with petrol on the journey. This interaction between the seen and the unseen (the scene and the un-scene) resonates with the inevitable invisibility of expanses of time and place in archaeology, where the 'deep time' of the past remains essentially obscured, offset by brief glimpses made possible by excavation.

The problem of grasping and expressing this 'deep time' has troubled the discipline since its earliest days. It was around 1860, with discoveries in the earth and life sciences – evidence from the fossil record, for example – that archaeologists were first confronted with previously unthinkable periods of time and the existence of a prehistory that forced a reconsideration of who we are and how we've lived. Not surprisingly, this spawned new anxieties about our place in time, and a 'fear of unintelligibility (of oblivion)'.[7] I've arranged to speak to Tim Murray, Emeritus Professor of Archaeology at La Trobe University in Melbourne, who has long been attempting to unravel the challenges of this 'deep time'.[8] In archaeological tradition, the problem has been dealt with by contrasting 'structure', which is derived from elements outside the lifespans of individuals, with 'event', which occurs within the lifespan of individuals and in which they have a part to play. These terms have more recently been challenged, as we'll see later, with a growing emphasis on a complexity of temporality that rejects such clear divisions, but this tradition is a useful starting point in its echoing of common approaches in fiction, in which elements outside the lives of the characters create a largely undifferentiated, unaddressed structure of absence, a kind of obscure backdrop to the more significant events that matter to the characters and are fully presented in the story.

I connect with Tim in his packed home office, the shelves behind him toppling with books and finds, and the warm, dim light and low ceiling giving the sense of a snug treasure cabin. I begin by asking about this relationship between deep time and the sudden revelation of a 'present', between structure and event. Tim has written about how long-term processes are not evident in the short-term record, and he leaps into an energetic explanation of how he sees the interconnections, helpfully beginning with the claim that 'all archaeology is fiction anyway'. Elaborating on this apparent fictionalization, he talks about how poorly we understand the scale and rate at which change takes place, and how difficult it is for us to extrapolate ourselves into a completely different time framework – hence the importance of the imaginative act. 'It's almost impossible to conceive of change of that scale', he suggests, drawing on astrophysics and palaeontology as useful touchstones for trying to think about the big sweep of time. He talks about the impossibility of capturing a 'present' in archaeological terms, giving an example from his own work on a site 2.5 metres deep covering a period from 6,000 to 35,000 years ago. As he explains, the smallest possible sample of material that can be tested from such a site is a 2 cm deposit, which will return a result of ± two hundred years, a time frame that embraces 'the entire white history of Australia'. Under these conditions, questions of past and present become obfuscated, and our view of time complicated: 'it's like something pixelating', he suggests. 'The more you refine chronologies down, the less you see'.

In view of this impossibility of locating any given 'present', evidencing a complete past, or even grasping the notion and implications of deep time, our conversation returns to how a process of fictionalization might intervene in trying to understand the interaction between event and structure. Tim's work has frequently addressed the debate in archaeology about the validity of adopting uniformitarian assumptions in an effort to make sense of the past – in basic terms, 'the scale and intensity of the influence of the present on our encounter with the archaeological past', how far it might be justifiable to assume the past was like the present, and whether we should apply our knowledge of the present to investigation of the past.[9] As we discuss these issues, Tim points out that there's inevitably 'an element' of fictionalization in the alignment and/or differentiation of past and present, proposing a choice between accepting that the past is completely unintelligible and can never be known, or 'a kind of fooling and fiddling' that results in an 'agreed-upon fiction'. Some archaeologists consider this inference-from-absence legitimate, but Tim sanguinely accepts that some within the discipline view such statements as 'heretical'. He nonetheless presses the importance of the new perspectives made possible by this act of imagination, the potential for an explicit embrace of a 'fiction' that allows for what he terms 'an immersion in the contrary'.

According to Tim, it's not only archaeologists who fail to adequately address and express the complexity of time. Fiction writers are not good at it either, he says, although he reads fiction widely, especially historical novels – every year, he re-reads all twenty novels of Patrick O'Brian's Aubrey–Maturin series of naval dramas set during the Napoleonic Wars. He makes an illuminating comparison, not between the writer and the archaeologist, but between the archaeologist and the reader: in understanding a work of fiction, he points out, the individual reader is forced to engage in an act of interpretation that fills in the gaps and silences inevitably left by the writer's handling of time. Just as an archaeological site can never reveal everything, so the reader pieces together facts, conversations, relationships, events, meetings and contexts – swathes of time passing – which have been excluded or eroded by the constraints of the novel form. As writers, we rely on our readers to make these efforts, to take on the imaginative leaps required to create sense from the text. An archaeologist's work, Tim suggests, can be viewed in the same way, the constant reading of the past depending on a sophisticated assimilation of time concealed, fractured or implied.

The rhythm of absence and presence – of time shown and time withheld – is shared then, at least at a basic level, by both the fictional and the archaeological 'plot', but our understanding and experience of time is, of course, more complex than simply the ways in which particular moments are expressed or suppressed. Much archaeology is preoccupied with understanding sequences – of objects, habitations, sites, cultures, civilizations. These sequences in turn are expected to reveal chronologies that act, in effect, as creative narratives moving through time. Sometimes these chronologies might be perceived as absolute, for example, when radiocarbon dating is used to date an artifact. On other occasions, the sequences can be more relative or implied: when stratigraphy is employed to analyse the succession, distribution and composition of geological layers, for example, or when a typological methodology is applied to organize objects into groups or series based on the observation of a perceived similarity between their physical characteristics. Whichever method is employed, and despite the range of materials being investigated, the common thrust is towards coding, harmonizing, and so understanding, time: 'Archaeology is, for all practical purposes ... in search of the perfect, coherent temporal ordering' notes the British archaeologist, James McGlade.[10]

In recent decades, however, this notion of the perfect temporal ordering has been disrupted to take account of the experiential nature of time, the disjunctions, discontinuities and uncertainties that disrupt a seamless narrative of the past. The assumption that evidence can speak for itself once it's fitted into an appropriate timeline – and offer only one justifiable narrative – has been challenged, with a growing understanding that archaeology is confronting a much untidier sense of time than might have formerly been expressed. This archaeology of multiplicity and simultaneity is memorably defined by anthropologist and archaeologist Rosemary Joyce as a 'congealment' of many times of many durations. When I speak to Rosemary, who is Professor of Anthropology at the University of California, Berkeley (and I'll return to our conversation in more detail later), she emphasizes how the idealized representation of time in archaeology as being sedimented is 'not real'. Instead of a neat series of layers or ordered chronologies that can be read as discrete and sequential evidence of the past, there is, she says, a 'mixture of traces … and entanglement', a back-and-forth, round-and-about mishmash of time that requires archaeologists to grub around in 'the intersections of temporalities'.[11]

This sense of timelines as provisional, ambiguous or simply inaccurate is particularly true for archaeologists investigating prehistoric sites. In this case – unlike working with traditional historical material, with a basis in documentary evidence – individuals remain unknown and unnamed; the sense of time is forged less by specific characters or roles than by collectives, communities, societies, traditions, cultures, landscapes or even regions. Similarly, the boundaries between apparently discrete activities, characters and stories may blur and merge, rather as they might when we're recalling or recounting memories. It's in this more dynamic interaction of time frames, this merging of stories and the temporal dislocation of memory, that we can see an obvious affinity with the manipulation of time, which we recognize as the basis of fiction.

This comparison is explored by the British archaeologist Mark Pluciennik, who points out that the understanding of some of the most familiar and fundamental pre-historic topics, such as the transition from the Mesolithic to the Neolithic Ages – familiar to us as the change from a hunter-gatherer existence to a more settled farming way of life – 'virtually demands' the adoption not only of a narrative form but also explicitly of story. For these kinds of archaeological subjects, as for fiction, Pluciennik points out, it's the construction of a viable story that is fundamental to successfully organizing material through time to elicit meaning: 'Out of the selective (re)description of objects, elements, events, conditions, and characters and the myriad possible relationships between them in time, space, and nature, it is the plot, the thread of the story, which emphasizes particular paths, possibilities, and plausibilities of the "characters" and "events" and which draws the text together as a narrative'.[12] But Pluciennik also notes that simply organizing objects, people and actions into a viable structure, and depending on this chronology to confer significance, fails to completely satisfy the demands of either archaeology or fiction. To fully grasp how the story sits in time, something extra is required, he concludes, an approach that nods towards Rosemary's more complex notion of 'congealment' and which Pluciennik describes as 'in some way *more* than a sequential and selective description of possible events'.[13]

So what might this extra element be, and how is it more? Pluciennik edges towards an explanation that focuses on the ability of archaeological narrative to 'bring potentially disparate events within an overarching framework and attribute a common meaning which is more than the sum of its parts', but how this common meaning emerges and why it can be claimed to be 'more than the sum of its parts' remains vague, suggesting a mysterious, ineffable process that appears to resist interrogation.[14] Despite this lack of precision, however, I think Pluciennik's argument is worth repeating because in this view, as I understand it, the 'more' lies in the recognition of commonalities and correspondences that enable us to see the connections in the 'potentially disparate'. This brings us back to Joyce's emphasis on traces and tangles and points to the complex ways in which writers conceive of, and readers experience, time in fiction: 'as something *more* than a sequential and selective description of possible events'. In our wide-ranging conversation, Tim Murray expands on and clarifies some of these ideas and, in so doing, re-emphasizes the links between archaeological and fictional time. Archaeology's 'temporal and spatial world' of logic and secure mensuration and objective reality is, he claims, 'mythic', the certitude of a linear time, 'entirely fictional'. In their place, he suggests, is a 'possibility space', perhaps the 'something more' that Pluciennik was reaching for.[15] It's this possibility space that embraces the inconsistencies and incongruities of time, allowing for repetition, accident, coincidence, serendipity. It emphasizes the brevity, intensity and uniqueness of the event while setting it within an 'overarching framework' that is larger, slower, more stable. It fuses activity, people and place. In short, it recognizes and manipulates the narrative time familiar in fiction.

Let's pause here for a moment to consider in more detail how we understand the principles of narrative time in fiction. As writers, what is it we do when we organize time in our stories? And how does the handling of time effect character and plot?

Writers have long shown a fascination with how we perceive time and especially how we can capture its essence in our writing. At the beginning of the nineteenth century, in his long autobiographical poem, *The Prelude*, William Wordsworth memorably wrote about 'spots of time', the lingering influence of powerful, often brief, moments of intensified existence which we experience as more full of meaning and more evocative than the long stretches of time that constitute most of our lives, and which he called 'ordinary intercourse': 'there are in our existence spots of time/That with distinct pre-eminence retain/A renovating virtue ... passages of life that give/Profoundest knowledge'.[16] This recognition that our sense of time fluxes, and that our brains register and record it differently depending on what we're doing, our distractions and our mood – and as such, that narrative time presents a particular challenge to the fiction writer attempting to tame it – has been further explored by a number of theorists. In 1927, Martin Heidegger published *Being and Time*, an influential philosophical examination of the ways in which we recognize and interact with time: he suggested that we experience it in multiple layers, including the datable, public and measurable version we mostly exist 'within', i.e. the time we experience in everyday life; a broader 'historicality' in which emphasis is placed on the weight of a longer sweep of the past, and in which actions receive their definition from their contribution and relation to history; and a 'temporality' that is the deepest, most personal level of our relationship with time, in which the 'plural unity of past, present and future' is dominant –

not unlike my sense of a unified time as experienced during the Cnip dig.[17] Around the same time, the Russian literary critic, Mikhail Bakhtin, discussed the influence to writing practice of what he termed the chronotope, which expressed the intrinsic connectedness of time and space and the different ways in which we respond to them depending on (literary) context, a process in which 'time, as it were, thickens, takes on flesh, becomes artistically visible; likewise, space becomes charged and responsive to the movements of time, plot and history'.[18] For Bakhtin, the use of motifs in a novel – repeated events, objects or places – helped to bring time to the fore and emphasize the transition from one temporal phase to another; he suggested that typical motifs, such as the road, the castle, the provincial town or the threshold, formed the building blocks for writing, acting as 'condensed reminders of … time and place'.[19]

It's helpful at this point, perhaps, to distinguish between ways of viewing narrative time as discussed by theorists in relation to human experience and the way we use it as writers. The two both connect and diverge. So as later theorists wrestled with the difficult nature of time and the challenge of expressing its role in our lives, those focusing on time in fictional narrative simplified the debate into a methodology for creative practice. An influential structuralist model proposed two layers, usually defined as 'story' – the chronology of actions and events as experienced by the characters – and 'discourse', the manipulation of that story by the writer, which shapes the reader's perception of what's going on (not unlike the counterpoint of 'structure' and 'event' that we have been considering in an archaeological context). This model is sometimes abridged to the 'what' (story) and the 'how' (discourse) of storytelling. These layers, the result of technical choices by the writer, are of course processed simultaneously by the reader, often as a seamless whole that seems to make sense of the complexities and discrepancies between them. They are also, much like in archaeology, nothing like the easily defined layers of an elegant *mille-feuille*. It can be unhelpful to think of them as distinct and horizontal, when more often they rest upon and against each other, interwoven and interdependent. Narrative time in fiction is by no means purely linear or sequential. It remains dynamic, reflecting the lively ways in which time exists within the imagination.[20]

Grappling with this imaginative time can be a writing challenge that throws up multiple oddities and paradoxes. In his study of moral philosophy, for example, Alasdair MacIntyre points out that as writers we're inevitably juggling the vivid 'present' of the characters within the story with the knowledge that, for us, the story has already 'happened'. This, he explains, sits in direct contrast to the way in which we live the narratives of our lives, in which the experience always comes before the recounting of it: 'Stories are lived before they are told – except in fiction'.[21] I would argue that there's a further complicating factor, too. While traditionally time in narrative has been viewed solely as a relationship between the past and the present, it seems to me that as writers we're also engaging with a sense of future implicit in the question of what we're trying to achieve in the reader who will – at some unspecified time in the future – be reading the story; they will also be casting the fiction forwards as they speculate on the what-ifs and what-nexts of the plot. As the writer, we're in the powerful position of existing outside or above the events we're recounting, allowing us to take them all in simultaneously and to hold past, present and future in the possibilities of the text.

As we can see, then, constructing fiction has much more in common with an experiential approach to time than the mere two layers suggested by Structuralism. Just as we cannot experience the linearity of 'clock time' in our lives, tussling instead with a ragged interaction of time/s where the past and future are contained (even if concealed) in the present, so in our writing, the temporal unity of the story can be deceptive. By the end of a piece of fiction, the reader needs to be able to have worked out some kind of chronology that satisfies the events that have taken place and the actions of the characters – the plot needs to have concluded (however openly) in such a way that the reader can grasp how the actions, situations and relationships laid out on the preceding pages come together – but getting to this point might well involve the fragmenting and distorting, stretching and compressing, even the misrepresenting, of time in the form of, for example, flashback, flashforward, condensed scenes, dream sequences, metaphor, sub-plots or exposition.

Fiction is very often, too, a thing of memory – it uses the memories of the author to bring it to life; it excavates the memories of characters to enable action and plot. And the way we access the past through memory is notoriously unstable. The timeline of our memories bustles and bends with inconsistencies and anachronisms; memory frequently conflates (consciously or not) acts, impressions and 'evidence' from different times. This unreliability – which might allow the writer a freedom, or at least a disruption, outside the constraints of real time – is, in turn, often reflected in the shape and progress of the fictional narrative. Like an archaeological site, memory is understood through fragments. Salman Rushdie makes the metaphor explicit: looking back on his own past, across a distance of time and space, he suggests that 'the shards of memory acquired greater status, greater resonance, because they were *remains;* fragmentation made trivial things seem like symbols … there is an obvious parallel here with archaeology'. As he notes, memory is like 'the broken pots of antiquity' – the past can sometimes be reconstructed from these bits and pieces, but such a reconstruction is always and inevitably provisional.[22]

> ## *Fragments*
>
> Go for a short walk and try to find a small object with a human history: a scrap of litter, a coin, a piece of clothing. When you return with your fragment, study it closely. Draw it and write a brief description, including material, size, form, where and when the object was found. Research as much as you can about the object and note the key points.
>
> Now consider how you might use this information to build a convincing contextual picture about this object in time. Does the object have a past? How do you construct this past? How much of this construction is dependent on the information you've gathered, and how much is pictured in the imagination? What is the relationship between the walk you went on, during which you found the object, and the object's previous history? How has your finding of this fragment changed its meaning? Does your memory of finding this 'trivial thing' transform it?

Narrative time in our writing, then, is often fluid and unpredictable; it can offer changes of pace and focus and add texture and multiplicity to the lives of our characters. It can alter a reader's impression of a world or landscape by showing how place exists in multiple layers of time (like an archaeological site) and how lives can connect, even when the conventions of time seem to separate them. At the most extreme, this can be dazzling and disconcerting.

David Mitchell's 2004 novel, *Cloud Atlas*, for example, interlaces six accounts from different characters, from a nineteenth-century notary to a herdsman living in a postapocalyptic future, in what Mitchell has called a 'Russian Doll structure' of interwoven narratives that presents each as an artifact of the next and tests our understanding of time.[23] Each protagonist connects with the others, across time and space: the early-twentieth-century letters from the second historical thread set in Belgium, for example, are later discovered by the 1970s Californian journalist of the third; the sixth and final protagonist, Zachry, watches the fifth story of a dystopian twenty-first century unfold retrospectively and holographically. Time in the novel presents a linear arc – we read from a past to a future – but also recalls Latour's spiral as we move back and forth through the interactions between the characters, suggesting the cyclical nature of human activity and the power of revisitings and repetitions.

Less contortionist manipulations can be more subtle for the reader to grasp but equally effective in the writer's struggle to convey the ways in which we experience time. If we look closely at a passage from Jane Austen's 1817 novel, *Persuasion*, for example, we can see how the narrative focuses on the instantaneous, contrasting the emotional power of the momentary – Wordsworth's 'spots of time' – with the tedious slump of the ordinary. Towards the end of the novel, Captain Wentworth writes a love letter to Anne during a visit to her home. In the midst of a room bustling with family and visitors, he scribbles his note and then pauses, we're told, 'the next instant' to look at Anne and distract her from the buzz of the surrounding chatter. Having folded and sealed the letter 'with great rapidity', Captain Wentworth has only the briefest opportunity to slide it in front of Anne as he leaves; Austen tells us how he glances at her, his eyes 'fixed on her for a moment' with a glow of entreaty. He then slips away, the entire act being only 'the work of an instant!' The reader's attention is continually drawn to snatches of time, 'a moment', 'an instant'. As the narrator keeps us waiting to find out what the letter contains, she emphasizes again the change in fortunes and emotions made possible in such a short but potent passage of time, repeating the word 'instant' for the third time in a few lines: 'the revolution which one instant had made in Anne, was almost beyond expression'. By contrast, these momentary but momentous exchanges are set against long periods of inactivity and emotional deferral: when we finally see the contents of the letter, we understand how Captain Wentworth has been waiting 'eight years and a half' for an opportunity to declare his love. Showing how time has gathered pace during the final ten days, in which he's been loitering in Bath to determine Anne's feelings, Austen again draws on the instantaneous, noting how he's been acutely aware of 'every instant' in his anxiety about losing her.[24] In the narratives of time laid out in the letter, Austen thus repeats the narrative of the novel, juxtaposing the slow period of everyday waiting, the imperceptible normality of time passing, with the clarity and intensity of the instant.

In Austen's comparison of the eight years since Anne and Wentworth's first meeting – the unnecessary and prosaic delay in love, the long period of regret, 'so many, many years of division and estrangement' – with the revolutionary possibility of 'the present moment',[25] we become aware of what Bakhtin identified as a 'new feeling for time' evolving during the eighteenth century, in which the long arc of character growth and the acquisition of knowledge, which is expressed in the linear and chronological, is set against the disruptive energy of the unexpected and instantaneous in which sudden revelation and change can occur.[26] In *Persuasion*, Austen clearly picks out these moments, offering them to the reader as if spotlighted. Repeating the word 'instant' in emphasis, they are contrasted with the everyday passing of time – which is studiously recorded through phrases such as 'the next morning', 'that night', 'for some weeks past' – and detached from the forward movement of the rest of the novel. Her use of free indirect discourse allows her to temporarily pause the author–narrator perspective, with its retrospective understanding and commitment to clear chronologies, in order to foreground the subjective experiences of Anne as heroine, recognizing and responding to the unique moment and the surprising turn of events it contains. By isolating such moments for special attention in this way, she effectively stops time for both the characters and the reader.

I have this passage from *Persuasion* in mind when I begin a conversation with Ian Armit, Professor of Archaeology at the University of York and the archaeologist who led the dig at Cnip that I joined all those years ago. I explain how Austen's use of multiple time frames seems to me to echo one of the ways in which time might be experienced in archaeology: a long arc of largely unvisited years or even centuries which remain hidden and obscure, punctuated by brief, vivid interludes that occur when a particular site or object is revealed during excavation – the dim understanding of Austen's 'many, many years' juxtaposed with the disclosure of 'the present moment'. He agrees that this slippage between different perceptions of narrative time is important to an understanding of archaeology: from his perspective, he says, the understanding of time is always 'a tacking between the broad and the small', a process which he considers integral to archaeological practice. He goes on to explain how his work is built on this relentless tension, a dynamic energy he describes as 'a constant swirl' drawing him in two directions, to both a long view informing his understanding of the broad context of a site and a close focus that is 'very, very specific' and centered on a brief moment within the larger arc. 'It's a knitting together', he says, 'of high-level theory and the evidence of material objects, of physical things, to understand and communicate how a society operated but also how a brief habitation, for example, might fit into the long view of what changes happen over time'.

This distinction between the abstract concept of chronology significant in theoretical reflection and the concrete, intimate physicality of the object as revealed on site strikes me as particularly helpful for the fiction writer charged with finding and expressing a lived experience of time passing. Ian and I discuss how the overarching 'meta narratives' of archaeology – the rise and fall of a civilization, for example – might provide a type of narrative structure akin to the plotting of fiction, where the writer (and subsequently the reader) is required to stand back from the everyday life of the character in order to place them in the wider shifts of community, society, nation and so on. Viewed this way, a character's 'meta narrative' might include, for example, her country's slide into political revolution, the social upheaval this causes and the calamitous effects on the economic and domestic lives on a broad community. Many sweeping nineteenth-century novels – sometimes identified as 'social novels' – present us with this kind of comprehensive overview in which the narrative adopts a wide lens through which to show time: Thomas Mann's *Buddenbrooks* (1901) chronicles the fortunes of a family over four generations, during which established habits, hierarchies and values are challenged by industrialization;

similarly, Thomas Hardy's *Tess of the d'Urbervilles* (1891) sets Tess's personal tragedy against the longer, more far-reaching decline of an ancient way of inhabiting and using the land. More recent writers have adopted the same approach. E. L. Doctorow's 2009 novel, *Homer and Langley*, for example, pits the reclusive brothers' enclosed lives against a long span of external events that allow the reader to move through time and history: twentieth-century wars, a flu epidemic, a New York era of gangsters and prohibition, civil rights protests and the physical transformation of the city beyond the walls of the brothers' brownstone house near Central Park. Memories, cars, clothes and newspapers – debris and treasure – accumulate in a cluttered labyrinth of material evidence that acts as witness to this extended chronology: 'It was as if the times blew through our house like a wind, and these were the things deposited', explains Homer in his narration, recalling the language of archaeology.[27]

Constructing narrative time in this way, from distance and with broad strokes, can make it appear seamless; the reader is unable to properly distinguish one moment from the next. Fluctuations and interruptions become invisible, just as all the years for which we have no archaeological evidence remain concealed and unknown. But within these 'meta narratives' that Ian identifies, I suggest that excavations can be viewed as scenes, as dramatic interludes which illumine the long view, in much the same way as a fiction writer pulls a specific event into focus. Attention is drawn to the material – to pottery shards, jewelry fragments, carvings, marks – and in so doing, the lives around this materiality become vivid and dramatic; time coheres around these objects and becomes visible. So the fiction writer steps into the broader arc in which her characters exist to show the revolution of the instant that Austen emphasizes in *Persuasion*. As writers, we dig our way from scene to scene, from surface to materiality, in order to understand and communicate our narrative. Our job, like Ian's, is to find a way through 'the constant swirl' of possible directions, interpretations and chronologies to what he's already described as 'the very, very specific'.[28]

With this common ground established, I ask Ian, tentatively, whether he considers any form of fictionalization to be important to his practice. He doesn't seem to object to the suggestion. On the contrary, he expands on the idea. He explains how his excavation reports usually include a discussion section, a speculative summary, in which the evidence from the site is hedged in more hypothetical – indeed distinctly fictional – terms. He emphasizes that it's not a strategy adopted by all archaeologists, but that he considers it important to recognize the 'imaginative leaps' that inevitably take place when you begin to ponder what most likely occurred in a particular place. When I ask him whether these imaginative leaps could be viewed as a fictionalization, he hesitates: 'kind-of', he says, and then expands: 'When you bring in theoretical work about society, region and period and apply it to an individual site, you *are* fictionalising in a sense'. He explains how archaeology, like all science, is a process of creating generalized models, in this case from groups of objects, but that these models exist in order to be refined and improved. He sees the archaeologist's role as making sense of all the elements intrinsic to the model, what he terms 'making the diffuse comprehensible'. As part of this process, uncertainties are identified, unknowns unearthed; time is inconsistently understood. It's in 'this attempt to fill the gaps', he believes, that the 'slightly fictional' emerges. He points out that as he brings to bear what is known about people and place on the objective evidence, as he fleshes out the material through a creative act of imagination, this conscious speculation – or fiction-making – allows him to raise new questions, creating an iterative process of discovery that often forces him to return to the archaeology. In this revisiting, he then finds he's able 'to see things differently to the first time round'.

I reflect on our conversation about seeing things differently over the following days. I find it interesting that Ian cited two authors as influential in his reading: Jonathan Raban and Bruce Chatwin. Both are writers of travel and the novel, often blurring the boundaries between genres and merging the lines between fact and fiction, the observed and imagined; they are writers of the journey and place, and especially of the passing of time. Chatwin's novel, *On the Black Hill*, has been called 'a masterpiece of temporal flow'; in the life story of the Jones twins in a farm in the Welsh borderlands, he takes full control of narrative time, 'giving over entire chapters to snits of time, whereas whole years will pass within a subclause of a trailing sentence'.[29] Writing in the *London Review of Books*, the poet Mark Ford noted that Raban skilfully responded to 'the different dimensions of contemporary reality'.[30] It seems fitting that these two writers, with their skilful and complex manipulation of narrative time, inform Ian's archaeology in some way, and in response, I look again at how we construct a sense of time in the fiction we write.

The writer's task is to fabricate and dramatize time. While the archaeologist is charged with unearthing, recording and understanding time as evidenced in the material record, the writer is required to conjure an apparently authentic present from nothing, to secure it to a convincing past, and to make this imagined moment a thing of fascination to the reader. In general, the more fully a fictional point in time is dramatized, the more space it takes up in the chronology of the plot and so the more weight it bears in the story: if we write the intense drama of a battle scene, for example, with all the details of the fight, dwelling on the clash of weapons, the cries of the combatants or the clamour of the crowd, the smell of blood, the internal anguish of the warriors, perhaps, and the triumph or disaster of the outcome, this brief but potent event will stand out as consequential as well as entertaining, signalling its impact on the rest of the story. The writer can't show every moment in a timeline and would not want to. The important choice then is how and when to make time count, which will depend, at least in part, on the nature of the story being told. Time suspended in the fury of my battle scene, for example, might be significant in establishing sympathy for my warrior protagonist and introducing the reader to the powerful antagonisms which shape my plot. In a traditional *bildungsroman,* the slow piecing together of a life is predicated on a belief that the longer something takes, the more invested we become in its outcome. Allowing the reader to inhabit the world of a close group of characters for many years, enables her to see ways in which they change and develop, their errors and successes, allowing her to care intensely about them. On the same basis, fictional series which extend the fate of a character, or set of characters, from novel to novel keep drawing the reader back to a world and time frame, implicating them anew in the fortunes on the page; a quest saga structured across generations and with an even longer backdrop provided by myth and legend – as is often the case with high fantasy – raises the stakes for both characters and readers as time progresses.

But the dramatization of time, perhaps paradoxically, does not necessarily require the sweep of ages, and in fact might benefit from a less ambitious chronology. In many ways, the writer, like the archaeologist, struggles to express what Tim Murray calls 'deep time'. How do you capture the passing of long periods on the page without resorting to generalization, vagueness or mysticism? How do you contain all the temporal complexities of a life within eighty thousand words or so of the novel form? In response to these challenges, many writers prefer the intensity of the moment, as we've seen in Austen's *Persuasion*. A more powerful dramatization often reduces the focus of the fiction to a few days, or even a few hours, drawing the reader's attention to the multi-temporal present in a character's head rather than a more conventional timeline of external event. To explore this technique more fully, I want to turn briefly (but perhaps inevitably) to the work of Virginia Woolf, a writer who uses time as a major device in her fiction, and whose writing was informed by a lifelong interest in archaeology and anthropology. In her novel, *Mrs Dalloway*, which takes place over the course of twenty-four hours in London in 1923, the reader is clearly confronted by the disparity between clock time – signalled by the chiming of Big Ben throughout the novel – and lived time. The restriction of 'real' time passing provides an intensification of thought and experience; time in the novel hardly exists as a physical entity but only as a means of cradling the dramatic inner life of the central character.

This sense of time as elastic and personal is perhaps even more evident in Woolf's 1927 novel, *To the Lighthouse*, which has been described as 'fashioned like an hourglass' with part one taking place over a vividly described afternoon and evening, a slim part two – called 'Time Passes' – encompassing ten years of war and death in which time is barely recognized, and the final part dramatizing in full the events of a single morning.[31] Our perception of narrative time is key to our reading of the novel, as Woolf and Mrs Ramsey, her central character, try to grasp the ways in which it affects us. During a lengthy dinner, in which the text moves back and forth between the polite chatter of the guests and their inner thoughts, Mrs Ramsey suddenly experiences a moment of intense emotional drama, even though it might be considered to anyone watching as a moment of stasis unworthy of attention. Dramatizing the unique experience of time to each of us as individuals, dependent on our inner lives and the context of the moment, Woolf observes how the experience 'partook of eternity ... in the face of the flowing, the fleeting, the spectral'.

> ## *The Long and the Short*
>
> Write a short fictional scene set at a kitchen table. The scene should be brief, no more than 500 words. A glimpse or snapshot. It might, for example, just be a description of what's on the table, or it might be a family drama taking place around it, or a quiet depiction of someone writing a private letter.
>
> Now write three more 500-word scenes at the same table but covering a period of years – perhaps 2, 5 and 10 years after the first scene took place. Pay attention to the material evidence and how it changes: what objects are important to each scene? What do they suggest about the characters or place the scene in time?
>
> Now consider how you are going to 'join' the scenes to create a narrative. What order would you organize them in? Do you need to write new material to join the gaps in time, or can the scenes stand alone, with the reader filling in what's missing?

The dramatization of time as a writer, Woolf seems to suggest, is about helping the reader access the complexities and depths of character, what she describes (in echoes of archaeology) as digging out the 'beautiful caves' below the surface.[32] In doing so, of course, what she emphasizes is the fragile and elusive experience of being human; our perception of time, as she exposes, is key to our perception of humanity. This understanding of time as an important element in our sense of self, in our identity as individuals and communities, becomes the focus of my final conversation with Rosemary Joyce. She emphasizes archaeology's role in defining, or at least suggesting, a flow of time we can understand, allowing us to grasp what it means to live now in this brief flicker we inhabit between, and dependent on, the past and the future. Central to this understanding, she explains, is the process of creating connections, bringing together 'diverse circles of participants engaged in attempts to understand the past'.[33] In this drawing out of connections and contexts, she claims, storytelling is 'internal' to the discipline, not only in fieldwork where the archaeologist makes 'piles of sediments into some kind of text' but also in lectures, videos, museum displays and exhibitions.[34]

This process, however, conceals the fact that, as we've seen, there are no such distinct layers in archaeology – as Rosemary emphasizes, 'the representation of time as sedimented is idealized, not real'. Grappling with the reality of a more muddled and complex temporality can make storytelling complicated. Echoing Tim Murray, she is clear that 'we don't have a very good notion of time', and it's here that she draws attention to the importance of dramatization. Rather than offering story as a simplification or linearization of time, she proposes it as a way of creating drama and in so doing, evoking a 'sense of being there', both in terms of the original events from the long past and during the excavation at a more recent past. This dramatization alerts us to a mixture of traces from temporalities of different durations and what Rosemary terms their 'entanglement', which in turn enables us to place ourselves alongside other participants from a range of different pasts, bringing us directly into contact with who we are by locating us in – and defining us within – a shared humanity. For Rosemary, it's this focus on understanding what it means to be human over time that is key, with story acting as a way of accessing and rendering this 'humanness'.

Rosemary returns throughout our conversation to the 'humanness' of time; her natural warmth and easy manner draw me into her argument about the importance of peopling the processes of discovery. She explains how the 'narration as running commentary', which was built into historical field practice and expressed through series of letters and diaries written on site, allowed this more complex and immediate notion of time to be present, but it has been lost, she suggests, in favour of a disconnected 'laboratory of the past' predicated on objectivity and the dry language of the journal article. This loss is significant, she says, because it places us outside a 'sealed container' and so removes archaeology from interaction with humans. She makes a telling comparison to the omniscient narrator in fiction, whose godlike perspective creates distance and in so doing is 'not necessarily very interesting'. In reply, I ask whether she sees archaeologists instead, then, more like the unreliable narrator popular in contemporary fiction, the deceptive 'I'. Laughing, she suggests there may be some truth in the comparison. 'We shouldn't be, but may all be', she concedes, and we consider how archaeologists, like writers – and especially unreliable narrators – choose to withhold some facts, electing the information considered appropriate for a particular site. While the archaeological process is faithful to the material evidence, Rosemary explains, 'many stories are possible from the same truths'. This multiplicity – of time and place, of stories and truths, of who we are – lies at the heart of the search for the human, which is intrinsic to both archaeology and the writing of fiction.

The discussions I've shared for this chapter have helped me better understand the ways in which we conceive of, and express, time in our lives as well as in our writing. I'm left with little doubt that there are significant intersections between archaeology and fiction in the handling of the past and its relationship to our perception of the present. Some of these intersections are immediately evident: as many commentators note, archaeology frequently begins (or ends) by telling a story of some kind, creating a dialogue between then and now, between the archaeologist and his interpretation; fieldwork, like writing, discards from the outset some meanings in favour of others, chooses which (and whose) story to follow, and directs attention to where meaning might lie. Both archaeologists and writers investigate the material artifacts of the past to try to reveal dynamics that might otherwise remain invisible. Other intersections are more contested and perhaps fruitful, particularly in the emphasis on the multivocal and elusive nature of constructions of the past. There is a valid comparison to be made, I would argue, between the novel and the archaeological site, both of which contain multiple, and sometimes simultaneous, temporalities but which, in addition, highlight how the fundamental nature of the object – whether it's a tool, a clay deposit, an heirloom or a haunted house – never belongs to a single moment but contains a jumble of disputed moments, years or even longer. While many archaeologists are wary of (or directly opposed to) speculation, I would also argue that an element of fictionalization inevitably exists in the imaginative act of placing people from the past in any kind of context and that archaeology shares with fiction a process of humanizing material evidence and conceptualizing human existence through time. For the archaeologist, a close investigation of the methodologies of fiction writing can help inform discussion about the strengths and limits of this process, and the tangle of times in which it exists.

As writers, the archaeologist's commitment to the material record reminds us of the importance of the object in time and how significance lies in observation, detail and comparison. Similarly, the discipline's ability to consider, and express, time as a 'thing', as a concrete (and catalysing) component in a site or theory, is a point on which to dwell. This reminder of its powerful role is useful when we're considering not only the construction of our fictions (the inevitable process of plot) but also the ways in which time, in all its forms, provides an essential underpinning for character and relationship, place and setting, object and subject. As Rosemary is keen to emphasize, imagining and understanding time – its physicality and its intangibility – allows us to reach some kind of knowledge about what it is to be human; as Gabriel García Márquez suggests in *Love in the Time of Cholera*, we exist both in time and outside it: 'the essence of a human being is resistant to the passage of time. Our inner lives are eternal'.[35]

2
Character/Genetics

Of all the techniques we juggle as writers, the crafting of vibrant, multi-dimensional characters is perhaps one of the most conspicuous, and the one by which success is perhaps most often judged. At festivals and workshops, best-selling novelists are pressed to reveal the secrets of effective characterization; how-to books and blogs attempt to unpick the mechanics of making a character come alive on the page. And at the root of this preoccupation is a simple realization: readers demand a great deal from the characters we create. They're anxious to know what our characters look like, how they walk, talk and dress, but also how they think and dream and interact with others, what drives and constrains them. Fiction is expected to lay bare inner lives that entertain and intrigue, that are beguiling, maybe amusing or perhaps troubling, often conflicted, certainly complex. Readers delight in watching as characters journey towards self-knowledge or are pressed to reveal concealed parts of themselves to others, as they blossom and mature, crumple and collapse, expose their flaws, failures and prejudices, or experience a fundamental change in their relationship to the world. And through this act of witness, the reader may also hope to understand something about themselves and those around them. Even if the setting is otherworldly and strange, the period unfamiliar or the action farfetched, an engaging character will contain and reflect essential elements of what we think of as 'humanness'. In this respect, the writing of character appears to be a deceptively simple exchange: the writer conjures as much of a 'real' person as she can and has them play out an interesting situation that then might be scrutinized by the reader. In turn, the reader temporarily buys into this fictional life as a means of experiencing something of the human condition.

At the heart of this exchange is the notion of believability. Can the reader *believe* in this character, at least for a stretch of a few pages? Does the character seem 'right', their actions and reactions authentic? Is there an inner life here that can be understood; can strange behaviours be assimilated? Under this weight of creative expectation, it's easy to think of fictional characters as extraordinary in some way, but of course what we're talking about is mainly ordinary people recast into story. The most successful fictional characters are usually the closest, at some fundamental level, to those we recognize around us. So in an effort to answer yes to all these questions and others, the writer aims for a 'truth' grounded in an intimate knowledge of ourselves, family, friends and lovers, people closest to us whose characters we consider identified and known. But of course, the building of character is not just about replicating a quirky relative. In search of an elusive combination of originality and veracity, we also scan through a highlights reel of memories and meetings and conversations, glimpses of people we bump into, anecdotes and second-hand stories, the bits and pieces we've gleaned about neighbors and colleagues and distant acquaintances, pre-loved portrayals from television or social media, half-memories of other fictions, details from news reports or local gossip. Evolving as a composite of these suggestions and impressions, the character finally enters the fiction as someone the writer and reader can agree is, at least for the moment, authentic.

So, is this ad hoc, instinctive process up to the task of creating character? Back in 1924, Virginia Woolf warned: 'Think how little we know about character'. In her essay *Mr. Bennett and Mrs. Brown*, she highlighted the uncertainties and ambiguities that were sure to dog the writer and outlined the 'hideous perils' that lie in wait in any attempt to capture the nature of another person in words.[1] But in the century since Woolf's essay, we have, of course, come to know a great deal more about character, and this knowledge necessarily informs the context in which we're writing. Alongside a personal, improvised construction of fictional character based on a hotchpotch of impressions, memories and imaginative leaps, we now have access to multiple ways of investigating, assessing and measuring who we are; the 'hideous perils' facing the writer have been rebuffed by revolutionary advances in a range of scientific fields examining the physical and psychological self. So as the perception of character is transformed by science, what does this mean for the writer? With such a bank of sophisticated knowledge in the public domain, is it easier to create a 'realistic' character and expect the reader to believe in them, or is the task infinitely more difficult?[2]

In this chapter, I want to address these questions with particular reference to the discipline of genetics, a field that has permanently recast our understanding of the self and significantly compounded the complexities recognized by Woolf. The international Human Genome Project, which ran from 1990 to 2003, identified, mapped and sequenced the human genome, determining the exact order of bases that make up the DNA molecule – identifying who we are at the most fundamental level.[3] The study of genetics, and its associated impact on neuroscience and psychology, has highlighted both our human similarities – we are all 99.9 per cent identical at DNA level – and the importance of our differences, as tiny variations in genetic interactions have been shown to have a far-reaching impact on how we behave and function. The idea of genes and genetics has become firmly implanted in the popular imagination, providing the basis for numerous books, film and games, while our individuality is increasingly reduced to, and tested by, DNA evidence; our sense of who we are is determined by quick tests for predisposition to disease or family relatedness, the right to pass border controls, the design of precision medicine treatments, or perhaps even a connection to a crime. I want to explore whether this increase in knowledge about, and familiarity with, genetic processes has brought us any closer to understanding the fictional character, or whether it has simply multiplied Woolf's 'hideous perils'. By talking in this chapter to geneticists about the nature of character and what this might mean for writers, I'm hoping to explore how the evolving science can – or should – impact on our writing of fiction. I also want to investigate what our understanding of the gene implies for a writing of fictional character traditionally predicated on the principle of malleability, a journey leading to transformation or epiphany, a life of evolution and disclosure fashioning an arc for the reader to follow.

In addition, I'm hoping to turn the tables to find out whether there are similarities between the way we think of character in fiction and how it's described and perceived in genetics. It's possible that there are no useful connections: when I began my search for geneticists willing to talk to me to inform this chapter, several declined the invitation, saying they saw no possible intersection between their practice and mine. Most geneticists are working in a 'hard science' context: the language they use is very different to the fiction writer's, and finding a way of talking about the concepts is perhaps the first stumbling block. But it's also true that most genetics research is closely focused on biology and medicine, applied to understanding how the body works and developing groundbreaking treatments for genetic conditions. Following the Human Genome Project, attention in molecular biology largely turned from the question of how genes mould certain traits or characteristics to attempting to identify those that code for particular diseases, so for some working in the field, the subject of this chapter is of minor importance, looking back to a discussion which has already been normalized and superseded. Nonetheless, I'm determined to persevere. With the particular emphasis on fictional characterization, and with half a century of genetic knowledge under our belts, I believe the issues around genetics and character might be worth a second glance. Despite the reservations of some of those I contacted, I suspect that there *are* interesting meeting points between the two disciplines. So I intend to test this contention in this chapter with the hope of understanding more clearly what character is and what it might be that makes a fictional character successful. Is reading and writing character more than simply reading and writing DNA? In the tangle of the biological, environmental and social, where do we find meaning about who we are?

The term 'genetics' was coined around 1906, with the word 'gene' emerging three years later, introduced by the Danish pharmacist and botanist, Wilhelm Johannsen.[4] At this point, no one could really define what such a word might mean, and there was no sense that it might transform our understanding of human biology. It was simply 'a very applicable little word', Johannsen noted, 'of no value to propose any hypothesis'.[5] By 1933, there was still scepticism about whether genes existed and if so, whether they mattered, with the American evolutionary biologist, T. H. Morgan, suggesting, 'there is no consensus ... as to what genes are – whether they are real or purely fictitious'.[6] But by the middle of the twentieth century, all such doubts had been dispelled, and it is now generally accepted that the individual gene is an intricate pattern of interdependent, often discontinuous DNA that can be used for building the multiple and essential proteins on which our bodies rely; genetics is firmly established as the foundational concept underlying, and unifying, biological understanding. The identification of the unique structure of DNA in the 1950s and the international collaboration of the Human Genome Project, with the aim of determining the exact order of the bases which make up the segments of DNA, further transformed the way we think about what human biology might entail.

In a quickly moving and often contentious field, the study of genetics provided significant insights into how our bodies work at a fundamental level, but it also raised questions. In many ways, sequencing the human genome proved to be a beginning rather than an end, launching a new series of problems rather than simply providing answers. Researchers discovered, for example, that humans express only about 2 per cent of their entire genome, which means that the majority – which was previously dismissed as insignificant 'junk DNA' – is not yet fully understood even though it is clearly instrumental to a complete knowledge of genetic material. Similarly, the realization that genes work in clusters – that they are composite rather than unitary, bundled together and functioning in interrelated groups or sets rather than as discrete objects – challenged any easy assumptions about how an individual's DNA might affect their life: each gene normally involves ten thousand or more of these interactions, and each human cell in turn combines more than 20,000 genes, so the possibilities and variations conceivable in any one of us are enormous. And among these ongoing puzzles and debates is one of particular significance to this chapter: how does genetic evidence sit with knowledge about our psychologies? At what point does biological make-up impact the actions, choices and emotions that we consider to be the building blocks of character?

Not surprisingly, these knotty conversations elicited some new – or newly pertinent – words. As writers, we tend to use 'character' as a catch-all term for the qualities displayed by the people in our fictions, but an evolving scientific language more accurately reflected subtle distinctions by designating specific terms to the various elements of our appearance and behaviours. These discrete terms can be helpful, so for this chapter, it's worth outlining each of them and the differences between them. The first is 'trait', which refers to an underlying, consistent and enduring emotional and behavioural pattern, often significantly determined by our genes and so described as 'heritable'. It includes observable and measurable details, like eye colour, height and weight (known as phenotypes), which can be up to 80 per cent or 90 per cent heritable, as well as invisible attributes, such as compassion, curiosity, altruism or scepticism, which can be 30 to 60 per cent genetic. Our preferences and quirks – whether we can solve crosswords or enjoy gardening, whether we thrive at team sports or in individual challenges, what subjects we select to study – are also the result of inherited genetics, but there is no single gene that 'creates' any ones of these traits; instead, each trait represents the organized interactions of several hundred genes.[7]

These behavioural traits are often grouped together into a broader understanding of temperament, which offers an overview of how our particular combination of traits makes us who we are. This temperament is, again, largely fixed and genetic: studies of identical twins have shown that they tend to have very similar temperaments even if they're raised apart.[8] Temperament makes up a key part of the self we project to the world, which is termed 'personality'. This is a tendency to respond in certain ways to certain circumstances and is quite likely to be the basis of how those around us perceive us; it was defined by the American psychologist David Funder as 'an individual's characteristic pattern of thought, emotion, and behavior, together with the psychological mechanisms – hidden or not – behind these patterns'.[9] Personality is unchanging, unique to each of us, and again, largely genetically determined; research has shown that our environment has very little enduring effect. This has led the psychologist and geneticist Robert Plomin to claim that factors such as parenting, family life and education ultimately 'don't make much of a difference', accounting for only between 0 and 10 per cent of our personalities; the only 'systematic, stable and long-lasting source of who we are is DNA' he concludes.[10]

This emphasis on the primacy of so many genetically determined aspects of our physical and behavioural self might prompt a heart-sinking moment for the fiction writer, whose task it is to offer the reader a sense of character development and transformation. If our traits are largely genetic, our temperament fixed and our personalities determined, then it might appear to leave little room for fictional manoeuvre. Fortunately, however, many scientists take issue with Plomin's claim that genetics is the only thing that matters (as we'll see later in this chapter). And in the dynamic area where genetics, neuroscience and psychology collide, each informing and challenging the other, we begin to see a more fluid picture of the individual. So finally, we come to the term 'character', which is generally taken to mean the total person, including all their traits and particularly their inner self, which is often connected to a moral or belief system. It's a term less commonly employed in genetic discussion than trait or personality, but it's here that we begin to unearth some of the possibilities which writers have traditionally found appealing. The elements that comprise character are those most likely to reveal themselves under duress or in the face of unexpected experiences, otherwise remaining shielded from view, either purposely or subconsciously. So for the writer hurling their characters into dramatic plot events, from apocalypse disasters to relationship break-ups, this idea that accident and calamity can force them to expose their inner self is promising. Perhaps most significantly, the notion of character also represents the parts of ourselves that we may have some power to change: our moral view, for example, may mutate with experience; our social attitudes might be abruptly altered by a particular relationship. In some ways, then, the term 'character' feeds into the traditional view of the fictional arc: while personality is regarded as largely immutable and governed by genetic heritability, some aspects of character can be malleable – although depending on your genetic make-up, this change may be easier or harder to affect.

The interrelation of these different terms shows the complexity of what we think of as character and raises questions about how we might present these layers of trait, temperament and personality in our writing of fiction. This is the point at which I begin a conversation with Dr Misha Angrist, Assistant Professor at the Duke University Institute for Genome Sciences and Policy in the United States. His 2007 book, *Here Is a Human Being*, discusses his experience as the fourth subject in the Personal Genome Project, initiated by Harvard University in 2005, and aiming to sequence the individual complete genomes of tens of thousands of volunteers in order to inform medical research.

His current work continues to explore the medical applications of genome research, but with an MFA in creative writing, he brings an intriguing dual perspective that I'm hoping will help me untangle some of the implications of the genetics debates for writers.

I'm not disappointed. Misha moves smoothly between discussion of scientific research to its political implications to the portrayal of genetics on the screen and in books. As an example of the difficulties in grasping how all these elements, and others, interact, he draws my attention to the 1997 film *Gattaca*, which he often watches with his students. With a starry cast including Ethan Hawke, Uma Thurman and Jude Law, it's a dystopian science-fiction portrayal of a future in which an individual's fate – from marriage to work to life expectancy – is predetermined by genetic selection. In the film, those subject to genetic unknowns as a result of natural or accidental conception, like the central character and narrator, Vincent Freeman (free man), are shunted into menial jobs and forced to declare their 'in-valid' status to potential partners. Misha admires *Gattaca*'s cinematography and admits the film is popular with his students, but, he suggests, it represents just the kind of 'failure of imagination' that continues to dog genetics and its portrayal in fiction: 'genetics is not unwritable', he argues, 'but it requires something more fully realized than just saying we're a product of our genes'. The idea of the genome as a reliable or total description of life itself, he explains, has evolved into something far more uncertain and radical. Too often, he says, social and political commentary overlooks these profound and sometimes quick-fire developments, and fiction fails to keep up. He makes a case for bold and demanding writing that grapples with some of the wide-ranging problems and implications being exposed by current research.

But where might this writing come from? In view of Misha's foregrounding of a more ambitious imagination, we discuss how genetics storylines have often been regarded as the sole province of speculative genres, shunted into a siding and labelled as strange, implausible or sensational. This is despite the fact that many of the situations first imagined by writers and appearing in fiction subsequently turned out to be prescient. Genetically engineered characters appear in Aldous Huxley's *Brave New World* published in 1932, for example, which tells us in its opening pages that all humans are manufactured to fit a particular role and born out of test tubes in 'The Hatchery'; ninety years later, genetic testing of embryos is now marketed as a potential add-on to IVF treatment. A misjudgement in genetic engineering propels the dinosaur plot of Michael Crichton's *Jurassic Park* (1990); in 2023, genetically edited animals were approved for human consumption in the United States. Margaret Atwood's 2003 novel, *Oryx and Crake*, juggles genetic manipulation with an intentional global pandemic concocted by a crack bioengineering team with obvious echoes in the debate that raged around the source of the Covid-19 virus. In Kazuo Ishiguro's *Never Let Me Go* (2005), human clones are created to provide organs for medical treatment; international scientists are currently working on cloning human tissue to treat diseases such as diabetes and Parkinson's.

These – and many more – are influential novels that have created scenarios that have later played out in a similar way in the real world, but for Misha, the issue lies in the sense of threat and doom which has generally attended them. Nearly always, he says, these fictions tackle the apparent menace of genetic research in the wrong (or careless) hands, and he finds something limiting in an approach that 'feeds into a narrow dystopian trope'. It's too easy for writers to use genetics as a springboard for perpetuating what he calls a 'tech Frankenstein ideal', a simplistic methodology in which characterization – and plot – predicated on genetics research creates a monstrous outsider, dangerous mutations or a society completely structured upon (and overwhelmed by) the single idea: genetics research leads to eugenics, which leads to disaster, in one form or another. In response, he proposes a more low-key and realist role for genetics in fiction. Rather than the grand sweep of *Gattaca*, for example, he outlines a story in which a character genetically prone to a common disease struggles to access treatment in an American system of ruinously expensive healthcare. As he admits, despite his close involvement with the Personal Genome Project, he's now largely disillusioned by, and bored with, personal genomics. Its promise of a 'cure-all medicine chest' simply hasn't happened, he says, nor has the apparently 'grand plan to democratize genetics', but these consequential real-life issues hardly break the surface of fictional representations.

In considering the evolution of genetic fictions, the literary critic Clare Barker presses for the more nuanced approach that Misha champions in our conversations, similarly moving away from the disaster scenario of speculative genres. The real potential, she suggests, is in looking beyond genes simply as vehicles of information to consider ways in which they allow us to construct a character that exploits a fuller potential based on what she identifies as 'other frameworks for genetic knowledge'. These 'other frameworks', she suggests, allow the writer to explore different and new ways of conceptualizing characterization in relation to the human genome, emphasizing the complex interactions of 'identity, heredity, kinship, health and human-environment relationality'.[11] Like Misha, she highlights the ambition inherent in this approach to characterization. In this way, she suggests, writers can fully explore the possibilities that genetics research provides by 'forging new ways of engaging with the self, the other, ancestry, kinship, race, ethnicity and the materiality of the human body in relation to their new genetic knowledge'.[12] While speculative fiction offers a vibrant space for inspecting anxieties and ideas about genetics, and for imagining consequences and alternatives, Barker's identification of a 'new genetic knowledge' suggests that the area is no longer only the product or concern of speculative fiction but a current which can inform all fiction, a powerful, wide-ranging and inescapable influence – particularly in our understanding of character.

Nonetheless, the collapse of the individual into fragments, such as sequences of DNA code, predisposition to height or hair colour, or susceptibility to disease, provides a challenge to the writer; it breaks up the sense of self and fractures the idea of character as a reliable site of development. The advent of sequencing technologies and their launch beyond the closed scientific laboratory – increasingly available and affordable in direct-to-consumer packages – jeopardizes the fundamental notion of the individual story, threatening to subsume it into vast genomic databases. In her analysis of the impact of genetics research on narrative, Lara Choksey highlights the difficult task of reflecting on characterization in these conditions, proposing that 'narrative in the age of the genome registers the disappearance of the subject of liberal humanism into algorithms – and as such, presents a crisis for character development'.[13] To counter this threat, she presses for what she terms 'transactional characterization' which moves beyond the certainties of evidence and identification towards something more difficult and radical, towards the complex palimpsest proposed by Barker.[14] Misha agrees that this kind of new perspective is required if writers are to fully take account of what genetics research means for our sense of self, but he recognizes the difficulty of adopting a more negotiable approach to characterization. 'Writers need to reckon with the speed of change', he says. 'If genetics knowledge is not the end-point but the springboard, what are we jumping into?' If genetics is about more than offering an easy shortcut for characterization in which everything is (pre)explained by a character's DNA, he suggests, then it becomes a complex negotiation of genetic difference and contested selves, which is difficult to render on the page.

The scholar and novelist A. S. Byatt drew a direct link between fiction and genes in the way both encapsulate and preserve important elements of the self: 'Stories are like genes, they keep part of us alive after the end of our story'.[15] Salman Rushdie, long interested in the intersections between science and literature, has used similar metaphors of genetics to express how fiction has become an intrinsic element of our humanity: the 'story instinct' he suggests, 'is hardwired in our DNA', making it 'essential to us all, whether we are writers or not'.[16] In *The Satanic Verses* (1988) he looks more closely at this connection between story, humanity and genetics in order to consider new questions about who we are and how we present ourselves to the world. Employing the freedom of a speculative form, he draws on magical realism to explore how personal (particularly traumatic) experience can result in radical changes to a character's DNA. At the beginning of the novel, Saladin Chamcha, an expat Indian and voiceover artist, falls from an exploding airoplane but is miraculously saved. Back on the ground, he's picked up by police and immigration officers and subject to terrible abuse; at this point, his body begins to change, growing increasingly grotesque. He sprouts horns and hoofs, develops thick hair and ultimately becomes monstrous and unrecognizable, 'a figure covered in mud and ice and blood, the hairiest creature you ever saw, with the shanks and hoofs of a giant goat, a man's torso covered in goat's hair, human arms, and a horned but otherwise human head covered in muck and grime'.[17] The treatment meted out by the police is shown to have a direct physical impact on Saladin, not just in the wounds and bruises on his skin but at a more fundamental level; the hostility, suspicion and hatred they direct at him is projected into his body so that he becomes identifiable as the outsider they fear, a visible manifestation of their prejudice. Furthermore, as Saladin is taken to hospital in the detention center, we discover that such an experience is not unique to him: a number of similar transformations have taken place as the bigotry, racism and violence experienced by the immigrants becomes written into their genetic code. Their physical appearance is no longer inherited or innate but constructed by those around them, radically altered by what is said and thought by others until they become the thing so described:

> there's a woman over that way … who is now mostly water-buffalo. There are businessmen from Nigeria who have grown sturdy tails. There is a group of holidaymakers from Senegal who were doing no more than changing planes when they were turned into slippery snakes.[18]

As the story progresses, the alterations to Saladin's appearance continue to accumulate. He takes on a devilish form, with Rushdie describing him as a menacing mythical creature: 'Chamcha had grown to a height of over eight feet, and from his nostrils there emerged smoke of two different colours, yellow from the left, and from the right, black. He was no longer wearing clothes. His bodily hair had grown thick and long, his tail was swishing angrily, his eyes were a pale but luminous red'.[19] His voice turns into a screech, and he's shown adopting animal behaviours, 'nibbling absently at his bedsheets'.[20] But he does not become an animal; he is able to debate his own monstrosity and what it might mean, and he continues to flail his way through tangled relationships, becoming reconciled with his father after decades of estrangement. Rushdie presents the animal and the human as intertwined and interdependent, and Saladin's sense of self as bound up in both. He negotiates the upheaval of all his experiences, past and present, to ultimately recognize a more stable familiar nature: 'Saladin felt hourly closer to many old, rejected selves, many alternative Saladins – or rather Salahuddins – which had split off from himself as he made his various life choices, but which had apparently continued to exist'.[21] By the end of the novel, when he loses the animal traits he's accumulated and is returned to a recognizable human form, Saladin's personality – the outward self – determined by his genetics is re-established. In this return, Rushdie's character seems to be echoing Robert Plomin's contention that 'Beyond the systematic and stable force of genetics, good things and bad things just happen … these random experiences don't matter much in the long run because their impact is not long-lasting. We eventually rebound to our genetic trajectory'.[22]

Discussing the human genome project, Rushdie's contemporary, Ian McEwan, pointed out that the research process of pooling the genes from multiple participants and merging them into a coherent sequence created 'just the sort of composite, plausible, imaginary person a novelist might dream up'.[23] In his novel, *Saturday* – published less than two years after the Human Genome Project produced the final sequencing mapping of the complete human set of DNA – he explores some of the implications of genetic research and its impact on characterization. Henry Perowne, *Saturday*'s protagonist, is a skilled and successful neurosurgeon who espouses a view of an unshakeable genetic character similar to Plomin's. He's interested in evidence, an account of behaviour and event 'that happens to be demonstrably true' rather than the complications of the fictions pressed on him by his daughter Daisy, a poet.[24] For Perowne, language and literature fall short in explaining the self; he prefers to rely on an objective worldview based upon an evolutionary frame of reference. (When the novel opens, he is reading Darwin.) This is a man 'in watcher mode', a distant scientific observer shown gazing at a plane crash from his bedroom window or peering from above on the activity in a London square or scrutinizing the intricacies of the human brain from the privileged god-like position of the surgeon.[25] When a car crash forces him into a more direct encounter with the unpredictable Baxter, he recognizes in Baxter the signs of Huntington's disease, the 'faulty cogs' that will ultimately undo 'the brilliant machinery of being'.[26] As far as Perowne is concerned, this genetic flaw is all he needs to understand about Baxter to understand everything.

Perowne's on-the-hoof assessment is correct: Baxter does have Huntington's disease. And as the Saturday of the title progresses, Perowne remains convinced that Baxter can be completely contained by this diagnosis. He recognizes the disease as 'biological determinism in its purest form', and no matter what behaviours Baxter exhibits as he forces his way into the family circle, Perowne attributes everything to genetic factors with no possibility of mitigation or change: 'it is written', he muses, 'No amount of love, drugs, Bible classes or prison sentencing can cure Baxter or shift him from his course. It is spelled out in fragile proteins, but it could be carved in stone or tempered steel'.[27] Despite this certainty, however, Baxter's behaviour *is* recast at the end of the novel, not through Perowne's neuroscience (although the final scenes show him operating on Baxter in a successful emergency procedure) but through the unexpected intervention of poetry in the form of Daisy's moving recitation of Arnold's *On Dover Beach*. It is this moment that upends what, until this point, might appear to be a pair of characterizations constrained by the rules of genetic science. Indeed, in his reading of this scene, the literary critic David Amigoni has suggested that as Perowne and Baxter listen to Daisy's recital, McEwan is allowing Baxter to break free of the restraints imposed on him by his genetic fortune, proposing instead a challenge to received meanings of genetic inheritance: 'Baxter's faulty gene becomes both a "switch", and receptor, for the appreciation of poetry … that Baxter and Perowne "hear" such different versions of the poem suggests that there is no universal genetic "programme"'.[28]

Playing out the science they describe, McEwan's central protagonists in *Saturday* collide directly with the implications of genetic research; the novel begins to pick a way through this new knowledge as a framework within which to build characters. But while some readers, such as Amigoni, have focused on the book's extensive use of literature and literary references to suggest an influence beyond the slavish power of genetics, those most grounded in the science have often balked at the characterizations. Nancy Wexler, an American geneticist and expert on Huntington's disease who was involved in the discovery of the gene that causes it, wrote a piece in *The Lancet* in response to the novel in which she expressed dismay at its 'pitiless stereotyping' of genetic disease as a thing of uncontrollable violence and oddness.[29] In my conversation with Misha, we talk about the character portrayals in *Saturday*, and he, too, expresses discomfort with the way the genetic context confines these characterizations to a single point of view, with their fictional journeys apparently determined from the outset. Perowne notes succinctly: 'our future is fixed and easily foretold', but Misha is troubled by this apparent simplicity.[30] As we discuss, our understanding of the nuances of genetics has progressed significantly in the twenty years since the publication of *Saturday*, and many of its approaches can now appear simplistic and outdated. Fiction has to keep track of contemporary debate, Misha emphasizes, which in terms of genetics means being alert and responsive to a rapidly changing field. 'It's too easy to say we are our DNA – the end', he says, emphasizing the importance of looking beyond the restrictions of this kind of formula if we want, as writers, to understand how character works.

Speculating on DNA

Imagine a fictional character. An unexplained accident has altered this character's DNA: they now demonstrate a physical change which is evident to those around them. This might be, as in the case of Saladdin, the growth of a tail or animal ears; it might be that they show symptoms of a disease or a change to height, weight or simply eye colour. Who was this character before the change, and what effect has the change had? How are they coping? Do they like the new reality, or does it alarm them?

Write a scene where the character goes home to their family for the first time since the change took place. How will they and those around them react? What implications will this genetic change have for their relationships?

Let's return briefly to the figures that, it's generally agreed, explain the influence of genetics: as we've seen, while most physical traits are highly heritable, behavioural traits are around 30 to 60 per cent inherited; we've also examined how environmental factors account for only 10 per cent or less of our behaviour. This means that around half of what we are is determined neither by genetics nor environment, neither nature nor nurture. Since we've also established that character, as distinct from personality and traits, emphasizes volition and is founded on elements such as morality and belief systems, which can be subject to change, we begin to see gaps in the apparent invincibility of the genetic apparatus. It's worth noting first that any variation in our individual natures is tiny compared with the almost overwhelming similarity in human nature generally, which, as we've seen, stands at 99.9 per cent. We are pretty much the same as everyone around us. But we know from our social interactions that small inflections of outlook, behaviour or attitude can make a difference to how we perceive ourselves and how others see us; it's these inflections that can be a promising starting point for the writer.

I've arranged to speak to Dr Kevin Mitchell, Associate Professor of Genetics and Neuroscience at Trinity College, Dublin. I connect with him in the blurred characterless un-place of the standard Teams call, but Kevin soon fills the screen with his enthusiastic eloquence, steadfastly passionate in his defence of what he calls 'fine tunings', the variations from a genetic standard that each of us demonstrates in our characters. He speaks fluently about how genetic constraints mean there will always be given parameters within which character develops – 'our brains', he reminds me, 'are not blank slates' – but the exact conditions that each of us experience are never repeated for anyone else: 'there's a randomness as to how our brain develops which leads to an idiosyncratic outcome', he says. He explains that we adapt to the world in ways informed by these 'fine tunings' unique to the individual, so that while our underlying genetic traits may be difficult to change, our behaviour draws upon learning and contextual experience, as well as the policing and judgement of those around us, creating an interplay between us and the world. Although there's no evidence that we can alter our underlying psychological traits, this interplay creates an active process by which those traits are expressed.

We discuss the importance of this interplay for the writer and how this dynamic interaction is often at the heart of effective characterizations. Kevin explains how our selfhoods remain a constant, 'making you keep being you through time', so advocates writing character as a balancing act between these constraints and the possibility of change, ultimately creating what he terms 'a continuity of self' in which we identify the satisfying, authentic characters we respond to as readers. Unconvincing characters, he says, change personality traits, which is jarring for the reader and makes no sense, 'like playing a game with no rules'. He cites Jane Austen's Mr Darcy, one of his favourite fictional characters, as a good example of convincing characterization: what Austen shows us in *Pride and Prejudice*, he says, is the possibility of growth in response to the reactions of those around us. So Austen creates a tension between the inherent and unalterable traits of Mr Darcy's reticence and introspection – interpreted by those around him as arrogance – and an ongoing process of learning and change driven by his circle's (and particularly Elizabeth's) response to his behaviour. Darcy himself admits to an instinctive 'propensity' to appearing cold and distant and appears to recognize the deep-seated influence of what we would now term 'personality traits': 'there is, I believe, in every disposition ... a natural defect, which not even the best education can overcome'.[31] But in the later chapters of the novel, he works to mitigate his natural reserve to show a warmth and practical kindness, which transforms his character in the eyes of those around him and the reader. This example, I suggest, shows how as fiction writers we can negotiate the tricky question of free will, allowing space for us to explore the nuances of character outside the restrictions of genetic determinism. Kevin agrees, pointing out that while there will always be prior constraints that are genetically determined, we're more than just a physical system making random responses to situations: we are what he terms a 'self with aims'. So, he explains, we are likely to actively select the environments we live and work in and the experiences we have as we each 'take ownership' of our character, developing habits through time that inculcate a self-awareness and making decisions which are informed by the cumulative effect of our previous choices. In this way, we maintain 'our core selves, balancing plasticity and stability to retain prior knowledge and adaptive habits while allowing new behaviors to be learned'.[32]

Kevin's research continues to emphasize our role as 'active agents' in our own fates; in our conversation, he reasserts his belief that we do more than simply act out a genetic pre-programme; he maintains our ability to make choices and the possibility of new behaviours. He takes issue with genetic determinists who insist that we remain passive while things just happen to us: in this scenario, he says, 'you disappear – you never have will in any moment'. Instead, he talks about a 'trajectory of life' based on the choices we make. He approaches the question of agency by highlighting how we actively select from these choices dependent on environments and experiences. When I ask whether it's valid to compare this trajectory to the traditional character arc evident in fiction, in which we witness a character's transformation in response to what happens in the story, Kevin agrees. The writer's task, he advises, is to draw out the implications of this interaction between plasticity and stability. Just like successful fictional characters, he says, we are clearly responsible for the choices we make, each of which emerges from the particular context in which we find ourselves. For the writer, he suggests, the priority is eliciting and articulating the situations and choices that allow a character 'the bandwidth to develop'.

> ## A word about character
>
> A 1936 study found 17,953 unique English-language words to describe personality or behaviour (Gordon Allport and Henry Odbert used Webster's New International Dictionary). This list was subsequently reduced to make it more manageable. But how many words can you use to describe your own character? Write a list, trying to find a variety of words to describe your reactions to a range of situations, moods and events. Some of these might be linked – for example, boisterous, loud, extrovert – but some might suggest a divergence – for example, boisterous, loud, extrovert, thoughtful, intellectual, depraved.
>
> How many of your words are linked to a particular environment or role? (e.g. talkative at home but reticent at work, motherly, efficient, hard-working). How many are linked to your 'self with aims'? (e.g. ambitious, creative, homely, sexy). How many of the same words would you use to describe family and close friends? Can you identify words that feel like stable descriptions, no matter what is happening to you, where you are or how old you are, and those which describe only certain situations or moments in your life? Now choose just three words from the list to define your key traits. What would they be and why?
>
> What are the problems with such a simple approach to character through words? And what are the advantages? Do we need to understand genetic process to give these words meaning?

In a rapidly evolving discipline, the question of whether, and how much, our environment and experiences might impact on genetics is at the heart of many contemporary debates. The initial conception of the gene was as something stable and predictable, responsible for a range of physical and psychological determinants, but some neuroscientists and psychologists now suggest that it may be more plastic than originally thought. While there is general agreement that the DNA sequence, as the basis of genetic information, provides the foundations of the self, recent attention has turned to how the gene operates, and in particular the role of the proteins that control how DNA is read by the cells. The traditional idea that a gene is immutable has been challenged by those who suggest it can be shaped by, and is dynamically interconnected with, environment. This research proposes that our life experiences not only influence our behaviour as Kevin has discussed, or potentially alter the personality we present to the world, but that they might also create change at a more fundamental physical level, within our DNA.

Some scientists have likened the process by which proteins interact with DNA to a series of signals which the body interprets as a prompt to turn a gene 'on' or 'off', becoming more or less active depending on need. This mechanism, known as gene regulation, is far more complicated than we can explore here, but is a normal part of our development: it enables the formation of differing gene patterns in different cells, ensuring that a brain cell is distinct from, for example, a liver cell. The study of these 'signals' is known as epigenetics, a term that defines a field concerned with the factors influencing a cell's ability to 'remember' past events, such as changes to the external environment or developmental cues. It's an approach that has come to the fore in the twenty-first century in a range of contexts, from child psychology to dentistry and well-being, often in a simplified form which captures the popular imagination by suggesting we can influence our DNA to unpick or ameliorate some of the genetic factors we're born with. For the writer, this possibility of change and agency can be very appealing, particularly when we're considering how our characters interact with, and are impacted by, the world we throw them into and the experiences we concoct for them. Several writers I've spoken to make use of epigenetics principles in their work, drawing directly on these theories in their building of character. So, for the remainder of this chapter I'm going to explore in more detail what the implications of this 'sub-genre' of genetics might be for characterization in fiction and whether it allows for new possibilities outside the constraints of genetic determinism.

Epigenetics processes can be very simple. Lying out in the sun and getting a tan, for example, involves changes in gene expression that increase the production of melanin, resulting in a darker skin tone. This is essentially an epigenetic process. More often, though, 'epigenetic marks' are significant in the earliest stages of gene development. These marks have been recognized in other life forms, like fungi and plants, for some time. The toadflax, for example, a yellow flower commonly found on waste ground and verges, can come in two varieties. These appear the same in every way, except for the shape of the flower, which is very different in the two types: one is hooded, like a snapdragon, and one is star-like. Each variant passes on its unique character to its offspring, which makes them appear genetically different, but in fact their DNA is identical. The variation is explained by epigenetics – physical change in the plant caused by ecological stress prompted by factors such as drought or soil condition.

Some scientists now claim that this kind of epigenetic change can also be seen in mammals, including humans, with an emphasis on the influence of prenatal experience and its ongoing effect into adulthood. Just as Rushdie shows some of his characters in *The Satanic Verses* becoming fundamentally altered by distress, violence and racism, so the principle of epigenetic marks proposes that trauma experienced in the womb can leave a kind of 'scar' on our genetic make-up. One example frequently cited is based on research into the children of mothers who were pregnant during the famine known as the Dutch Hunger Winter of 1944–5, when the Nazis blockaded food supplies to the Netherlands. It was found that this next generation ended up heavier than average in later life, as well as experiencing higher than average rates of obesity, diabetes and schizophrenia. The implications of this, some researchers suggest, is that their bodies remembered, and later reacted to, the environment to which they were exposed in the womb.[33] It doesn't seem clear, yet, how this process might happen or what exactly is occurring at a genetic level, but the epigenetic argument proposes that early childhood trauma causes an alteration in gene expression so that 'terrible early childhood experiences change certain physical aspects of the brain' and 'a triggering event continues to have consequences long after the trigger itself has disappeared'.[34]

In explaining the implications of this epigenetics theory in her book, *The Epigenetics Revolution*, Nessa Carey compares epigenetic regulation of gene expression to a film script on which various people – writer, director, actors – scribble notes at different stages of production. She explains the epigenetic process as a series of such accumulations, each remaining legible as the script passes from hand to hand: 'Different cells have the same DNA blueprint (the original author's script) but carrying varied molecular modifications (the shooting script) which can be transmitted from mother cell to daughter cell during cell division'.[35] Some research even suggests the life story of this genetic script may be significantly longer than Carey outlines, with older annotations leaving their mark in the margins. These experiments claim, controversially, that epigenetics might be responsible for transgenerational inheritance; that is, changes in DNA that occur in subsequent generations rather than the one directly affected. At its basic level, this theory proposes that something which affected our grandparents could now be showing up – for the first time – in us, including diseases that have responded to environmental factors in previous generations.[36] Studies with mice have shown that those with stressed mothers, for example, are much more likely to demonstrate increased levels of anxiety; in humans, the children and grandchildren of Holocaust survivors demonstrate a higher prevalence of PTSD and other psychiatric diagnoses than control groups.[37] While disputed in mainstream epigenetics, these transgenerational principles create an intriguing new twist in the traditional nature–nurture debate: rather than each new embryo building its DNA from scratch, this approach would suggest that certain tags remain in place from earlier generations, so events and experiences from the past can put down markers that continue to stain the present.

This view of epigenetics, which proposes that the on/off switchboard of signals can be activated by psychological as well as physical experiences, is a controversial one, and there are many in the discipline who express scepticism. Kevin Mitchell draws on the suntan example to suggest that we would be foolish to adopt an epigenetics approach more widely: 'That's an awfully long and complex road from genes to psychological traits. The idea that we can change those traits by altering the expression of some genes in adults – like getting a suntan – is therefore pretty fanciful'.[38] But for the writer, the idea of a malleable gene can be appealing, suggesting a new freedom for shaping character and raising some tantalizing questions. With this in mind, I've arranged to speak to Brigitte Nerlich, Emeritus Professor of Science, Language and Society at the University of Nottingham, who has researched the ways in which epigenetic ideas – and the language they've inspired – have been adopted beyond the core 'hard science' of genetics. Like Kevin, Brigitte expresses caution. She's critical of how epigenetic research has been adopted by so many commercial interests – especially wellness industries – as a way of giving people an 'illusion of control over their body' and warns against accepting a 'few very hyped-up studies' as evidence for some of the claims made about epigenetics: 'it has crept into popular consciousness and in the process the science got pretty corrupted', she says. She explains that while an agreed definition of epigenetics as environmentally caused and trans-generationally inherited seems to have evolved in the social sciences, she feels this consensus is 'built on shaky foundations', especially since geneticists and biologists are still divided about what epigenetics might mean. She also highlights a surge of garbled claims and inaccurate metaphors in popular culture that skews our understanding of epigenetics, exaggerating and over-simplifying messages about the dire consequences of, for example, certain kinds of diet or stresses in pregnancy, and 'potentially creating unrealistic expectations'.

Nonetheless, Brigitte says she understands why this concept of epigenetics can seem exciting, especially in its promise to 'throw away the shackles' of genetics. We discuss how this buzz of freedom might be appealing for writers and how a focus on fluidity and change can be alluring, especially as it appears to propose an element of control over who we are and hence over the characters we're creating. In response, she talks about the difficulties of finding adequate ways to express the nuance of epigenetics and how challenging it would be to show any kind of relationship between a character's development and the epigenetic processes to which they might be subject. She doesn't accept a determinist view of genetics but echoes Misha Angrist in pointing out that 'talking about scientific determinism is easy but to talk about the complexity of a dynamic variety of genetics is really difficult'. So while Brigitte rejects pervasive determinist metaphors, such as the genetic 'blueprint', she explains how difficult it is to find a more apt linguistic expression that captures a necessarily fluid approach: 'you're always working at the edges of language and meaning', she says.

From her comfortable study, with its bright garden window and colourful textiles, Brigitte offers a wide-ranging and sympathetic discussion of genetics, emphasizing the complexities, uncertainties and unknowns by returning several times to this idea of 'edges'; she talks about gaps and bridges. Her preoccupation with glimpses and connections prompts me to think about 'postmemory', a term that can be used to discuss fiction dealing with traumatic events, such as war, where the writer has no direct experience of the subject but draws on a collective memory filtering from the past: the word was coined in the early 1990s by the American critic Marianne Hirsch to describe 'the relationship that the "generation after" bears to the personal, collective, and cultural trauma of those who came before – to the experiences they "remember" only by means of the stories, images, and behaviors among which they grew up'.[39] So, for example, Elif Shafak's 2023 novel, *The Island of Missing Trees*, is set in Cyprus, a country divided by a border between Greece and Turkey and shaped by years of violence and ethnic conflict. Shafak underpins her story with the idea of inherited pain and silence, exploring the ways in which families with traumatic histories might transfer experiences of suffering and grief from one generation to another. Her teenage protagonist Ada 'had suspected that she carried within a sadness that was not quite her own', a feeling she interrogates in the context of science classes at school and their explanations of DNA. Ada comes to suspect an influence that we might recognize as transgenerational epigenetics: the question 'burning in her mind' is whether it's 'possible to inherit something as intangible and immeasurable as sorrow'.[40]

Talking about her novel, Shafak expands on these ideas. She explains: 'I've always believed in inherited pain. It's not scientific, perhaps, but things we cannot talk about easily within families do pass from one generation to the next, unspoken … it's left to the third generation to dig into memory. I've met many third-generation immigrants who have older memories even than their parents'.[41] Shafak's work sits in a long tradition of literature interested in, and shaping, languages of inheritance, analysing what is passed on, what lingers and what is forgotten, and how we are marked by what has gone before, described by Hirsch as 'traumatic fragments of events that still defy narrative reconstruction and exceed comprehension'.[42] Viewing epigenetics in this context, we can perhaps see how it feeds into notions of postmemory and writers' enduring fascination with traces of the past, working at the same kind of 'edges' Brigitte has identified: 'Postmemory does not aspire to neat and gratifying conclusions but rather aims to leave audiences with the unease of discovering that history – above all the history of events of extreme violence and suffering – leaves loose ends and gaps that no account is able to tie neatly together and fill'.[43]

In epigenetics, similarly stubborn loose ends and uneasy gaps persist, often becoming more rather than less apparent as research progresses. As Brigitte points out, this is a young field, still under construction, 'a field in flux, and a very complex one at that'. The 'plasticity of the field itself has to be acknowledged', she says, meaning that we need to be alert to an 'array of metaphors' which advance frequently conflicting interpretations of epigenetic evidence (or lack of evidence).[44] As she highlights, genetic research in general, and a focus on epigenetics in particular, is still only beginning to understand how our genes dictate our actions and shape our choices, and some tantalizing questions remain for the writer in search of a character. Not least of these is how far we can exploit the idea of transgenerational influences. Current research raises some provocative possibilities, suggesting that even Shafak's third-generation 'dig into memory' might end up being a conservative view of epigenetic inheritance: the Icelandic neurologist and geneticist, Kári Stefánsson, proposes, for example, that 'one of the big questions' soon to be resolved is whether we can inherit a thought. 'Is the way you think passed down from your mother and father?' he asks, suggesting a new direction for the literary staple of the dysfunctional family.[45]

While the conversations in this chapter have edged towards an understanding of character as pieced together, an assembly of traits and experiences, of past and present, body and behaviour, it is the inevitability of genetic constraints that remains constant in considering who we are. From the writer's point of view, these constraints should perhaps be viewed as an advantage, providing a structure within which to work: whatever we put in front of the characters we create and whatever experiences they live through, our task is to show the precious core of their natures that remains intact and that readers will recognize as authentic. Kevin Mitchell brings this challenge into focus when he highlights the way in which character is shaped by our past habits, our current decisions and the demands of genetic inheritance, these fragments melding into a continuity of self: 'You, right now, in the present, are just the momentary avatar – the representative in the world – of a self that stretches from the past to the future', he says.[46] In this sense of multiple temporalities we glimpse the discussion of the previous chapter and so the links between our fictional characters and the narrative time in which they exist. These characters *do* have room to act unexpectedly, to react idiosyncratically, to behave in response to the moment, but this immediacy has to exist within, and be set alongside, a much broader sweep of time rooted in the consistency demanded by genetics. Recalling the interaction of event and structure we explored in conversation with archaeologists, the writer's approach to character becomes in this way a negotiation of the fleeting and the intrinsic, dependent on an interaction with time. As the literary scholar Jerome de Groot points out, genetics research has demonstrated how our bodies exist both in 'deep time' – a far past – and in the present, 'both palimpsest and also a solid, contemporary living object ... DNA is something that is now and not-now ... self and other'.[47]

This view of human character as 'multitemporal, conflicted and conflicting' reaches to the heart of how we write it on the page.[48] Traditional plotting urges us to make our characters make choices and in so doing create conflict, which in turn builds a better characterization. The good news is that current genetics research mostly shows that these conflicts seem to be inherent and that choices still matter – maybe even for several generations to follow, if transgenerational epigenetics is to be believed. Perhaps most significantly, an awareness of the genetics debates reminds the writer of the limitations as well as the possibilities of choice, creating a friction that allows characters to blossom. For many writers, it's working in this space at the limits of possibility that brings characters to life. Haruki Murakami, for example, describes the point at which a character's choices exist in tension with imposed limits as a crux, a charged moment when they are able to 'break free of the writer's control and begin to act independently ... the characters take on a life of their own, the story moves forward by itself'.[49] As genetics research progresses, our understanding as to how far our behaviour is a question of – and product of – choice and how far it's predetermined will continue to be refined, offering rich ground for writers working at the heart of this crux.

But what about fiction's influence on genetics? Is there any way in which our writing of characters can impact how geneticists view their field or conduct their research? I think this is trickier ground. When I raise the question during my discussions, the responses suggest that creative work inspired by, and interrogating, genetics research is viewed as completely separate from – and irrelevant to – the 'hard science' research itself. As Misha Angst highlighted, numerous works of fiction have pre-empted genetics discoveries, creating an imaginative reality for possible breakthroughs before they actually happened, but any sense that fiction might somehow contribute to serious genetics research activity remains beyond the pale. Brigitte Nerlich points to two interconnected problems: what she terms a 'blindness' on the part of natural scientists, which can mean alternative and creative research tools are rejected, and a language barrier between disciplines. This barrier, she says, can 'prevent thinking' by making it impossible to communicate ideas effectively; ceding ground on language, she suggests, can be interpreted as losing an element of control over ideas, too, which some scientists can find alarming. 'We need to look at the language clash', she says, 'and how we can go beyond the clashing'. While some works of fiction can catalyse discussion around genetics research and its impact – she cites Michael Crichton's 2002 novel, *Prey*, as a 'cultural bombshell' of this type – any grasp of specific fiction techniques, such as characterization and what this might mean is, she suggests, a step too far. For now, then, perhaps the important thing is to continue the conversations with the aim of finding constructive points of similarity, challenging ingrained language habits and proposing change, offering the possibility that the craft we understand as writers of fiction might become embedded in the DNA of genetics research.

3
Narrative Structure/ Architecture

My geography teacher at school was a short, likeable man with sprouting ginger hair and a stash of popular jokes. He was enthusiastic about weather fronts, oxbow lakes and measuring the distance on maps with lengths of string; in our discussions of urban spaces, he introduced us to the concept of 'lines of desire'. For me, this has been a phrase that has stuck, revisited every time I encounter the scruffy paths marking the quickest route between two points, living histories trodden into grass or mud or snow. I became a serial observer of these modest pedestrian transgressions. I liked their egalitarian nature, the way they cock a snoop at planning schemes and park keepers, knowing and claiming space as a communal experience. But later, a curious linguistic jostle also sent me back to those geography-lesson discussions: these lines of desire became associated in my mind with the notion of reading between the lines. In this tangle of lines on the path and the page, I identified a commonality of spontaneous participation; both drew attention to the ways in which we butt into constructions fashioned by others, providing a reminder that what we make and write is inevitably subject to a web of social interpretations, to time and change and unexpected intervention. The pedestrian sneaks across a patch of grass to reach the bus stop just as a reader presses her interpretations between the words on the page.

This conjunction between lines of desire and reading between the lines also firmly established in my mind a connection between architecture and writing, and the ways in which both carve and constrain form and structure.

In this chapter, I intend to explore this connection in more detail, with a particular emphasis on how both disciplines contend with space. As in other chapters, my concern is with the technical decisions we take as writers and the complex processes that coalesce in the making of fiction. There are, of course, numerous literary examples in which architectural structures emerge as characters, contributing to plot, signalling meaning and acting as more than mere backdrop. Utopian and dystopian fictional worlds are frequently predicated on the powerful image of a menacing city, such as Batman's Gotham City or the 'future' Los Angeles of *Blade Runner*. Franz Kafka's castle in the novel of the same name rises inescapably above the village, a symbol of inexorable bureaucracy but more significantly, the antagonist in K's futile struggle for recognition, respect and companionship. The nineteenth-century literary Gothic, which summoned an aesthetic of dark, claustrophobic spaces and rambling ruins, frequently featured the medieval architectural style (or its new iterations) of the same name: Edgar Allen Poe's *The Fall of the House of Usher* (1839) includes many of the quintessential elements of what became recognized as Gothic fiction, in particular, a decaying and haunted country house, which acts as a metaphor for the human body and which crumbles and sinks as the family destroys itself, both a literal place of horror and a symbol of trauma and death. In Aravind Adiga's *Last Man in Tower* (2011), a shabby Mumbai tower block stands testament to an 'absolutely unimpeachably pucca' way of life that is passing, a neighborly, harmonious community being picked apart by new developers.[1]

There are many more examples, of course: stepping into an authentic and detailed built environment is a pleasure and preoccupation for many writers and readers. But this chapter is not about literary buildings and the role they might play.[2] Instead, I am taking as my starting point a recognition of what has been described by the architect and academic J. Kent Fitzsimons as a shared project, the proposition that 'writers and architects share an underlying project: to produce sense by tracing the contours of imagined human action'.[3] His emphasis on contours suggests both physical and imagined shaping, a bounding and moulding of spaces that contain intuition and understanding, a mutual goal that he defines as 'sense'. With this shared project in mind, I'm setting out to discover through my conversations how writers and architects in search of this human action conceive and construct space in their work, whether fictional processes have a role to play in shaping the conceptualization of these architectural spaces, and why (or if) thinking more like an architect might be helpful for the writer.

Architecture, that most demanding of visual forms, has always concerned itself with writing. In the first century BC, the Roman architect Vitruvius recognized the importance of expressing architectural ideas and practice in text and promoted a particular writing style, noting that 'you don't write about architecture as you write history or poems'. His demand that vague premises and clumsy language be set aside does not, these days, appear to separate architecture from creative writing, but rather to bring them together; his rule that ideas be 'condensed and explained in a few, crystal-clear sentences' provides a useful maxim for those of us trying to master prose fiction.[4] More recently, early-twentieth-century Modernist architecture found a partner in Modernist literature and avant-garde poetics: as many critics have noted, architecture and poetry of the period both attempted to explore structure and the meanings inherent in, or implied by, form. In this back-and-forth of practice and ideas, built and written expression often took inspiration from the other. A few decades later, perceptions of new construction in post-war Britain – from motorways and planned towns to tower blocks and social housing – were filtered through literature that brought projects thoroughly into the public realm, animating the social and political context from which they emerged and aiming to shape, complicate and lay claim to these new emerging architectures: in his poem 'Going Going' (1972), for example, Philip Larkin bemoaned the bricking-in of England to create 'the first slum of Europe'; in J. G. Ballard's 1975 novel *High Rise*, an apocalyptic tower block drives its inhabitants insane. Today, the dialogue continues: science fiction, in particular, has been recognized as 'a site for architects to stretch out into the breathtaking scope of all that can be imagined, beyond that which can be realised', while the august international journal, *The Architectural Review*, still continues to publish poetry;[5] the Courtauld Institute's 2011 conference on architecture and poetry was prompted by a recognition of shared ground in 'concepts of beauty and utility, of personality and indexicality, of inscription and graffiti and of memory and temporality'.[6]

The literary scholar, David Spurr, re-emphasizes this process of exchange, suggesting that architecture and literature sit comfortably 'in relation with one another' and noting that:

> Architecture, as the art of building, gives concrete form to the external world according to the structures of imagination; whereas literature, as the art of written language, gives symbolic form to the same world. In their respective manners architecture and literature are potentially the most unlimited of all art forms in their comprehension of human existence itself, and this fact alone justifies the task of putting them into relation with one another.[7]

The dialogue that Spurr identifies between the concrete and the symbolic foregrounds writing as a mode of making, reminding us that both the architectural and literary imaginations are about conceptualizing, expressing and capturing an interaction with people and places grounded in experiential, not just theoretical or imaginative, encounter. Both activities have always been mediating presences in our ways of living, reaching for Spurr's 'comprehension of human existence' and raising fundamental questions about what human existence might mean. But while comments such as Spurr's suggest a lively reciprocity, which the American architect and artist John Hejduk has identified as 'thought provoking, sense provoking, and ultimately life provoking', the long-standing interaction between architecture and fiction remained rather obscured until the emergence of what became known as 'narrative architecture' in the mid-1908s.[8] This formalizing of a theoretical approach explored how principles of narrative might be applied to the interpretation of buildings, and in so doing necessarily drew on elements of story. So, narrative architecture can refer to the 'stories' apparently evident in a structure, or the ways in which form or decoration might represent ideas, or how our interaction with buildings might be understood as a form of narrative. Proponents of narrative architecture recognize the importance of imaginative methodologies and not uncommonly draw comparisons between the writing of fiction and the design process: 'Fiction is unavoidably part of the architectural process; when conceiving a building there's always a speculative projection into the future', claims the American art historian Véronique Plesch, for example.[9]

In some buildings, the narrative elements can be obvious to the eye, made literal by the use of symbolism or decoration, which render visible both purpose and the underlying systems from which this purpose emerges: cathedrals, airports, romantic parklands, for example, all clearly signal what they're about and how they're meant to be 'read'. Such narratives have often been politically driven, linked to a desire to promote a particular ideology or belief system: the Stalinist architecture of mid-twentieth-century Russia acted as an aesthetic representation of the power of the state; the figurative decoration on Gothic churches was intended to operate, at least in part, as a storybook for a largely illiterate congregation. Walter Benjamin discusses the narratives made plain by commercial arcades of nineteenth-century Paris, which he views as fantasy constructions of burgeoning consumer capitalism, dreams of luxury and domestic bliss writ large in architecture of light, glass and iron.[10] My first conversation for this chapter is with Gordon Grice, a Canadian architect who has spent many years designing theme parks. These are openly constructed, he explains, on a brashly promoted story that he terms 'a fictional re-making of space'. He traces how story is thoroughly embedded in the complete design process, from the initial briefing of an overarching backstory about place and history to 'get the design team working in the same direction', through advertising and brand development to a visitor's engagement with the site – arrival and orientation, entertainment, eating, buying and finally heading home. This trajectory, he says, 'follows the rules of storytelling – build up, conflict, resolution'.

Other commentators have explored similarities between architecture and fiction by highlighting correspondences between the building and the book. The British architect, Nigel Coates, makes a direct comparison between the two, suggesting that buildings can be viewed as containers for emotions and meanings in a similar way to works of literature. Here he begins to touch on ideas of space as distinct from structure, discussing how imaginative engagement allows the users of buildings to assemble physical space 'into a personal construct' in much the same way as a writer and reader negotiate a fictional space in the object of the book: ' ... the physical nature of architecture makes it comparable to the physical object of the book, which sits between the author and the reader', he suggests, claiming that 'architecture needs now more than ever to connect through function and with fiction in equal proportions'.[11] This idea of an architecture embroiled with meaning has proved influential, becoming an integral element of some architecture courses; the design process is often recognized as a series of layering complementary (or sometimes competing) narratives of a project – in the text, diagram, drawing, model, construction – and many architects now choose to work with notions of story and storytelling as part of the design and build process.

There are also, however, many architects who argue that architecture is never about anything other than itself, that it just 'is'. They warn against becoming entrenched in worn metaphors of narrative that simply distract or misinterpret: 'give me the thing-in-itself, and not an obtrusive narrative', pleads Robert Venturi.[12] Adrian Forty takes issue with the idea that buildings can have 'character' and raises questions as to how a building can carry meaning and exactly how such a meaning might ever be discerned. Architecture, he contends, can 'represent nothing beyond its own immediate presence'.[13] Recognizing this ongoing debate, and inevitably overlapping in places with discourse about the value and validity of a narrative architecture approach, the discussion that follows considers not so much how buildings might be made to 'mean' something beyond the physical evidence they provide, nor whether architecture is required to tell a story in order to be successful, but rather what shared processes might be at work when architects and writers construct and express space.

As noted above, Nigel Coates highlights the significance of space throughout his discussion of narrative architecture, and in fact identifies it as an element unique to architectural practice, and so beyond the reach of fiction: 'buildings can be invested with narrative content by the architect in ways that are only possible through the medium of space', he argues. 'Having both substance and void, content and relations, space is a medium ready to soak up associative meanings'.[14] But Coates' suggestion that space necessarily requires physical expression, needing substance in order to acquire meaning, is challenged by others who look at notions of creating and interpreting space more broadly. Gaston Bachelard's seminal 1958 work, *The Poetics of Space*, explored archetypal images of domestic space in both 'real' and literary buildings as a way of understanding the imagination. More recently, the writer and scholar Giuliana Bruno returns to the comparison of the building and the book that Coates explores, but from the other side of the fence: she examines ways in which the book – and more pertinently, the story it contains – is like the building, rather than ways in which buildings might be read as books. In her description of the construction of her writing, she examines how the resulting book becomes a complex imaginative interaction of spaces, acquiring 'the substance and void, content and relations' that Coates distinguishes. Chapters are assembled, she explains, 'like the floors of a building ... The reader, moving from one part to the next, as in the architecture of a building, may notice repetitions and variation'. She envisages the reader constantly and physically progressing through the text, and in this act, the book coming together as though being built: 'Certainly there is an ascending path to be found in reading this work, as there is in most buildings ... it contains its own representations in the threads of its fabric, holding what has been assigned to it with every passage ... '[15]

As I consider this synergy, I arrange to speak to Pedro Gadanho, an architect and writer who has worked as Director of the Museum of Art, Architecture and Technology in Lisbon and Loeb Fellow at Harvard University. Pedro is keen to stress that, like Giuliana Bruno, he comes to this discussion from the opposite entry point to Coates. Rather than the movement through space being used to create some kind of narrative in a building, he says he's interested in 'how we can translate architectural knowledge into fiction and how we can use fiction to express ideas about architecture'. He talks about the Beyond project, in which he brought together a number of successful architects to write short stories. One of the prompts for the project, he explains, was the feeling that there existed a large accumulation of architectural research and knowledge, as well as innovative interactions with science and technology, which was being lost, neither translated into architectural projects nor transmitted through other means. So he began to look at what might happen if this research was reinvented as fiction. When I ask him about what he sees as the strengths of Beyond, he is clear that architecture gains from an interaction with fiction, in particular allowing for 'deep thinking'. By importing notions and approaches from creative writing and literature, he says, architectural thinking can move from the dry and academic to be 'richer, denser, more evocative'. He points out that buildings can easily be bland and abstract, so that fiction 'offers an unusual alternative to the rigid concerns of functional and technical suitability faced by architects', allowing for something more 'conflicting, intricate and manifold'.[16]

I find my conversation with Pedro inspiring and encouraging. Viewed from the perspective he promotes, fiction is firmly positioned as more than just a tool for looking at the history and theory of architecture, or as a means of foreseeing possible building features or uses. He describes a dynamic interaction, a 'way to have another dimension' that situates fiction and architecture as shared practice investigating a fascination with space and its potential. He often uses fiction, he says, rather than standard architectural description, in the design and development of a project because it 'creates an evocation' and is a way of 'bringing ghosts into the space'. I enjoy his metaphor of 'ghosts', suggestions of characters – as yet not fully formed – moving through imaginative spaces, making those spaces real and in turn, growing more substantial. Throughout our conversation, he places an engaging emphasis on the value of the imaginative act for its own sake, presenting this act as a thing with physical shape and presence, a voluminous, multidimensional space.

In the construction of a piece of fiction, these contours of action (to borrow from Kent Fitzsimons) are fabricated by the writer for characters to inhabit, experience and move through, not just cityscapes or cafes, offices or homes but psychological and emotional spaces charged with possibility as much as event. The imaginative realization of these spaces is essential to the fiction's success, the writer tasked with conjuring them from nothing, finding a language that renders a physicality to the characters within the story and the readers outside it, in the absence of any concrete or tangible marker. When this is successfully achieved, the effect can be striking: 'Have you ever had the feeling while reading a novel, a piece of nonfiction, a poem or a short story, that you were inside a structure built, knowingly or unknowingly, by the writer?' asks the Italian architect and writer, Matteo Pericoli. 'I don't mean the reader's natural process of imagining and visualizing the locations described in the text, but the clear sensation of being immersed in a space – a literary space – built by someone else'.[17]

Such fictional spaces exist on more than one plane, of course: in the writer's imagination, on the page, and in the reader's mind. In moving between these planes, the constructs are subject to interpretation, destruction, reconstruction, change. In most cases, the best the writer can hope for is that they make the language work in such a way that the reader can share and explore the space created by the text, allowing for an imaginative leap which will, at least in some important respects, approximate what the writer had in mind. Alice Munro likens this process to entering a house or 'an enclosed space', the reader acting as visitor, poking around, discovering and adopting the space and being changed in turn by what they find:

> wandering back and forth and settling where you like and discovering how the room and corridors relate to each other, how the world outside is altered by being viewed from these windows … you can go back again and again, and the house, the story, always contains more than you saw the last time. It also has a sturdy sense of itself of being built out of its own necessity, not just to shelter or beguile you.[18]

This process of, and interaction between, discovery and recurrence is echoed by Pedro Gadanho, too, as he discusses the uneasy but beguiling process of subjective exchange, which creates an innate link between architecture and fiction. Architects, he says, are always conceiving of a certain use for a building, which is subsequently, and inevitably, subverted by the actual users who may find an unexpected or totally different purpose for the space in the same way readers entering the fictional house described by Munro experience 'how the world outside is altered by being viewed from these windows'. This re-imagining and repurposing – recalling the crisscrossing of desire lines with which we began – makes the original construct 'more ambiguous', he says, affording the building 'a second life with multiple interpretations and meanings'. In this way, he suggests, architecture echoes the experience of the novelist, in which the writer's intentions are openly negotiated by the personal responses of the reader.

As writers, we're accustomed to (even if we don't always understand) this exchange with the reader who draws on both the text on the page and the space between and around it – the reading between the lines – to share in, and simultaneously reconstruct, the nature of the fiction. But what is it about the essence of the spaces we create in our fiction that allows this negotiation to take place, and is this interaction really the same as the three-dimensional, and very practical, experience of repurposing a building? In architecture (as in drawing and sculpture), space is a recognized tool, a powerful entity in its own right with resonances and repercussions: art and design consider the impact of negative space, for example; the interplay between form and space is at the heart of architectural thinking. But how might this preoccupation with space be meaningful to the writer, who is clearly not working in three dimensions, and barely in two; where the only physical space available is that between words or lines on a page, often dictated by the basics of syntax or the demands of the publisher? Is it reasonable to claim that space is as important a tool in fiction as it is in buildings?

In his influential examination of how we each lay claim to public spaces through a network of histories and relationships, Michel de Certeau uses the example of stories to consider the importance of movement and place. Just as we might walk through the city, experiencing a series of physical spaces, he says, so stories, are fundamentally spatial: ' … [they] traverse and organise places, they select and link them together, they make sentences and itineraries out of them. They are spatial trajectories … Every story is a travel story – a spatial practice'.[19] De Certeau goes on to explain how all our everyday activities, from crossing the street to consuming news reports, are 'narrated adventures' doused in the language and practice of space. Just as we've identified how fictional space is different to architectural elements featured in a story – the castle, cabin or stately home acting as setting – so de Certeau contends that these 'spatial trajectories' are separate to the idea of location, or place, which is 'ultimately reducible to the *being-there* of something dead'.[20] Rather than simply 'being-there', static and predictable, this concept of space is dynamic, requiring the intersection of a number of 'mobile' elements, including time and direction, which create passage, transgression and transformation. In another echo of my preoccupation with desire lines/reading between the lines, de Certeau claims that 'the street geometrically defined by urban planning is transformed into space by walkers', but also by the act of reading, and the practice of writing ('a system of signs').[21] In a similar vein, the Bakhtinian theory of chronotope, as we've seen in the first chapter, has both a temporal and spatial dimension. For Bakhtin, space (like time) is not an abstraction but an active, physical form 'of the most immediate reality'; as the writer works this space into something with presence, it 'becomes charged and responsive to the movements of time, plot and history'.[22] Rather like de Certeau, then, this is a vision of space as vigorous and imaginatively substantial, intricately bound to, and acting as a catalyst for, the ways in which fiction is conceived and constructed.

But what might this space look like? What does it mean for the writer to be working with a spatial element that is both real and imaginary, literary and visionary? It was similar questions to these that began to nag at Matteo Pericoli. Speaking to me from his studio in Turin, in front of a heavy wooden counter loaded with jars and paintbrushes, he begins by saying that the notion of space is a 'gigantic issue', not just for architects but for writers, too – and indeed for our ways of seeing the world in general. He describes himself as a non-architect, having 'let go' of the discipline in 2010; now, he says, he approaches ideas about architecture 'through the back door, or a window'. It was when he was invited to give a workshop at a creative writing school in Turin at the same time as he was moving away from architectural practice that he began to explore how writing works, and in particular how writers imagine space. Bringing his architectural experience to the question, he asked students to respond to short stories or novels without using words, instead building architectural models that might act as visual manifestations of each piece of fiction. The intention was not to be literal, creating a diagram of plot or a replica of structure (in fact, the single rule of the workshops was 'we mustn't replicate any location, object, setting, building, and so on, described in the text') but to capture the essence of the fiction in architectural form:

> And in a text, if you were to discard the words, what would be left? We talk about literary structure, emotions and feelings, and about how we can translate all this into proportions, light, darkness, solids and voids. We discuss spatial relationships, repetition, refection, sequence, transparency, tension, pacing, chronology and so forth. Any architectural question is answered from a literary point of view and any literary issue is addressed by a

spatial idea. There is no room for arbitrary moves. Any decision is guided by the interpretation of the text. We do not engage in any form of architectural criticism; we do not talk about styles, periods, traditions—just space.[23]

To further develop these ideas, Matteo founded The Laboratory of Literary Architecture, which explores writing as architecture and poses entertaining but demanding questions such as 'what makes a story stand?' When we talk, he explains how he considers the transition from architecture to writing to be a natural progression; he sees the drawn line as a 'precursor' to the written word, with ideas bursting through the 'ceiling of language', most often through the act of reading.

Matteo returns to the importance of reading and the reader several times during our discussion, openly placing it at the center of his thinking: too often, he says, architecture and creative writing have misunderstood the process of creativity and who is the active and passive agent. Writing and reading are both, he says, fundamentally about 'how you manage your time inside a space', but it's the reader, he claims, who is frequently the dynamic partner with the 'highest potential' for creativity; echoing Munro, he discusses how it's in the act of reading that we go into and through fictional spaces, using sensory experience to enable us to understand them. He explains how one of the purposes of the laboratory project was to give physical form to this reading experience, creating a three-dimensional representation of the 'wandering back and forth and settling' that Munro describes. But the activity of the Laboratory is also, he emphasizes, about reinstating the senses, and particularly the need to touch imaginary space/s. Space, he suggests, 'is not a story to tell, it's a story to live'. This element of tangibility is important, he says, because once you think of writing as about shape as much as content, 'it's a revelation'.

Matteo talks about the particular significance of suggestion to both architecture and writing, made evident in the way they construct meaning from glimpses and hints and 'things we don't think we've heard'. In the Laboratory, he makes explicit these shared devices in the two modes of practice: 'we discover how many of the challenges that writers face are similar to those of architects: How should different strands of narrative be intertwined? How can chronology be rearranged in a plot sequence? How is tension expressed? What do certain narrative sequences and omissions convey or mean? How do characters connect?'²⁴ He describes the process of writing as an excavation and is clear that what finally emerges for him is a physical, as much as an imaginative, space. Drawing on an extended metaphor to try to explain this materiality, he uses the example of translation to describe how language can create a 'skin' around this space – during the process of translating a work of fiction from one language to another, he says, this skin is taken off and put back. Below the skin, the spatial reality of the work remains untouched, something 'way more' than style or a particular language. As architectural comparison, he uses the example of the Pantheon in Rome, 'its monstrous empty space and its open eye hovering above'. He uses the term 'read' to explain how we understand the materials it's built from and, most importantly, how they act to 'define emptiness' in the same way the words of a text define the 'sensation of dynamic space' they contain.²⁵ This metaphor of writing as both skin and underlying space, as a thing accommodated, but not defined, by words, is a powerful one, which he described in more detail in a piece for *The New York Times,* re-emphasizing the link between the two modes of expression:

> In architecture, once you remove the skin – the "language" of walls, ceilings and slabs – all that remains is sheer space. In writing, once you discard language itself, the actual words, what's left? Thus we also work toward the questions that architects, knowingly or unknowingly, must always address: how does one design and build using emptiness as a construction material? How do we perceive space? And how does it affect us?²⁶

Drawing a Story

Take a story you know well – either one you've written yourself or something you've read several times – and draw the shape of it on a blank piece of paper. Start with a general sense: is it rounded or spiky? Symmetrical, elongated, disordered? How do the different characters and events connect, overlap or dissociate?

Now think about details. Would this 'story space' have decoration, and if so, what? Are there a series of internal spaces within the overall structure? You might also like to consider other questions such as: does this story have a colour? what texture would it be? is this story space viewed from above or below, through windows or doors or tunnels?

There are a number of fiction writers with architectural training, most famously, perhaps, Thomas Hardy, the son of a stone mason and builder who was articled to a Dorset architect at the age of sixteen. The Turkish Nobel laureate, Orhan Pamuk, also studied as an architect in Istanbul, leaving before graduation to become a writer – writing, he has claimed, gave him a richness and freedom that his inquiry into Modernist architecture did not permit, allowing him to sit 'with tradition and with those who refuse absolutely to bow to rules or to history. I am sitting with things born of coincidence and disorder, darkness, fear, and dirt, with the past and its ghosts, and all the things that officialdom and our language wish to forget'.[27] Many other writers, even without any formal training in architectural practice, have shown a fascination with how it might inform their work. The cityscape, in particular, has proved rich ground, with its tension between permanence and change. Arundhati Roy, for example, speaks about her fascination with Delhi as a place in flux, a 'never-ending story', and draws attention to the importance of 'physical space' in her description of her 1997 novel, *The God of Small Things*, as 'a novel with characters who appear and disappear, shaping the physical space around them'.[28]

As we've seen, science fiction settings commonly test possible urban futures, particularly in terms of the city and conurbation. In the second half of the twentieth century, for example, a new wave of science fiction engaged with ideas of vertical living as a response to social and structural change, often taking to extreme what was being witnessed in the rebuilding of real urban spaces, as can be seen in the title of Felix C. Gotschalk's 1975 novel, *Growing up in Tier 3000*. A flourishing field of geography, planning and urban studies now uses such fictional speculation, particularly science and cyber fiction, as a means of theorizing, again drawing attention to cognitive, psychological and imagined spaces as much as physical design: 'through its use of estrangement and defamiliarization, and its destabilization of the foundational assumptions of modernism, [fiction] provides a cognitive space in which to contemplate future spatialities'.[29] Italo Calvino's novel, *Invisible Cities* (1972), is a work that frequently features on the reading list for architecture and urban studies courses; its portraits of fifty-five cities (all of which might be read as portraits of aspects of Venice) have been used as both models and warnings for the urban professional, as they 'call into question many planning milestones (e.g. control, purpose, model, balance), fostering an original reflection on the limitations and potentials of planning practices'.[30]

Invisible Cities can appear piecemeal and stuttering; it is apparently disordered, filled with incongruities, fantasies and contradictions. But looking more closely, we see how the complex and unconventional structure facilitates nonlinear reading, the multiple directions contained by a symmetrical and rigid framework – in effect, the novel creates a convergence of intricate and challenging spaces accommodated within a larger and ultimately more coherent space (or perhaps the 'skin' described by Matteo Pericoli). In this way, Calvino and his narrator seem to be mirroring the experience of the city on the ground, the collision of soft and hard surfaces, of building and space – walking through a city is both a random imaginative encounter with space and a more rational experience of finding our way – but also addressing Matteo's questions about how we experience and express literary spaces. Calvino admitted his fascination with structure and form, noting that 'the architecture of my books has a very important place, perhaps too important'; in a work such as *Invisible Cities*, the fictionalization of space is thoroughly entangled with built environments, writing with architecture, the boundary between the book and the city elided.[31]

Despite – or perhaps because of – examples such as this one provided by Calvino, the concepts of space discussed in this chapter can be difficult to view distinctly on the page or analyse in terms of writing technique. The spaces of fiction (as distinct from its buildings) are largely constructed, as we've seen, by evocation rather than description and definition, made real in the mind of the reader in the cumulative effect of gaps and suggestions, betweens and beyonds, the 'wandering back and forth' identified by Munro. Nonetheless, in an attempt to better understand how we might fashion these spaces in our writing, and what effect they might have, I'm turning to a short story by Jorge Luis Borges, *The Aleph* (1945). Here, the narrator (a fictional Borges) recounts a repeated encounter with a house in Garay Street, Buenos Aires, a house he has visited many times to meet with his deceased lover, Beatriz Viterbo, and where her family still live. Borges gives precise details of time passing throughout the story; his account is waymarked by constant details such as 'one Friday morning', 'two Sundays later', 'on the thirtieth of April 1941', as well as the language of arrival and departure. But he does not describe the house at all; the narrator's visits over the course of twelve years are pieced together to create an intangible space, emotional as much as physical, haunted by Beatriz and the narrator's fractured memories of his time with her.

The house on Garay Street remains unpictured and featureless, but as the story progresses, the nature and understanding of this conventional domestic space, and the equally conventional tale of unrequited love, is radically challenged. One of the epigraphs Borges attaches to the story is a quote from *Hamlet* – 'Oh God! I could be bounded in a nutshell, and count myself a King of infinite space' (ii.2) – which focuses the reader on the potential of an imaginative space distinct and emancipated from physical constraints. So, as Borges continues to pay his visits and grow closer to the family, he is made aware of a mysterious thing called an aleph, a tiny orb situated in the pit-like cellar under the dining room. This aleph appears to allow the unpredictable and concurrent experience expressed by Hamlet;[32] it is, Borges is told, 'the only place on earth where all places are – seen from every angle, each standing clear, without any confusion or blending'.[33] With the aleph, Beatriz's cousin tells him, he will be able to 'babble' with every image of his lost love simultaneously in a miraculous expansion of time and space. All he needs to do to access this experience is to lie on his back in the dark and focus his attention on the nineteenth step of the stair leading from the house above – suggesting that all we need to do to access a world of infinite possibilities is position ourselves accurately. The cousin warns that failure to witness the aleph after taking up this specific location will be owing to the narrator's 'incapacity'; he blames a personal inadequacy (of vision or patience or imagination) rather than raising any doubt about the aleph's existence.

But the narrator manages to install himself in the cellar correctly and is indeed confronted with the powers of the aleph; at the heart of the story is a single long sentence in which he attempts to describe the experience. Here, he notes, 'begins my despair as a writer'. The psychological, conceptual and emotional space into which he enters through the aleph, a space grounded in, but exceeding, his knowledge of the world, is both intangible and indescribable. He does his best to capture the enormity and totality of the encounter for the reader, describing both the universal and the particular, from 'a silver cobweb in the centre of a pyramid' to 'all the mirrors of the world', 'equatorial deserts and every one of their grains of sand' and 'the multitudes of America' to 'some obscene letters' that Beatriz had written and the dust and bones of her remains. But his list of the strange and wonderful things he witnesses inevitably falls short. Both language and architecture (the story and the house) prove inadequate and unstable (the house is knocked down after Borges' final visit).

This crucial long sentence, the skin of the space made substantial through the aleph (to borrow again from Matteo Pericoli) is structured around the verb '*ver*', to see, which Borges employs forty times. The pattern of repetition, usually combined with the first-person pronoun (I saw), reinforces the idea of perception and the elusive nature of experience; this mysterious multiplicitous space filled with wonderful things, it suggests, is not so much inherent to the physical world but rather brought into being at the moment the narrator witnesses (or imagines) it; seeing, imagining and creating become conceptually interlaced in the 'infinite space' of the aleph. The winding sentence, divided into a series of shorter clauses, creates a container for the narrator's – and the reader's – imagination, the hull within which each of the new visions expands and hovers in space; the highly structured paragraph paradoxically allows for the chaotic profusion of visions within it, much as Calvino's carefully constructed framework in his novel facilitates the variety of his invisible cities.

Other writers have used a similar technique to equally powerful effect. Consider, for example, the notable passage in George Eliot's *Middlemarch* (1871–2) which is also constructed as a single long sentence, in this case holding the multiplicity of spaces, palimpsest of histories and clamoring visions of Rome that confront the impressionable young Dorothea Brooke. Concluding *The Aleph*, with a series of questions, Borges challenges the reader to believe in the kind of potent multitemporal expansion that overwhelms Dorothea but which is essential, he proposes (as does George Eliot) for a fully human experience of the world. Language, the story seems to conclude, will inevitably offer constraints; able to do little more than set out a series of places and things to be described, it proves incapable of capturing the complexity or, essentially, the simultaneity that the aleph offers. What the narrator sees through the aleph is a spatial phenomenon, all things and all times contained discretely, but the narrator's account is necessarily temporal, setting out each of the wonders one after another. Reading, however, need not be temporal. Once the reader has finished the story, they can contain and visit it in its entirety, fashioning for themselves a synchronous, multidimensional space that accommodates all the possibilities of both the aleph and the text. So, Borges suggests, the writer, like the architect, must begin with a constraining reality but in the interchange with the reader can make possible the ultimate space of the imagination.[34]

> ## *Skin and Space*
>
> Think about the external appearance, the skin, of your home. What is it made from? What size and shape is it? How does the light fall? Where are the entry points? How is each side different?
>
> Now consider the internal space. How is it defined, by corridors, windows, stairs, floors, etc.? How is it punctuated, by furniture, decoration, etc.? Where does the light fall? What is the sound of it? How does it feel?
>
> What happens to the internal space if you change the skin? Imagine your home with a completely different external appearance – your top floor flat is now a bunker underground, for example, or your square house in an urban street is now a soft round blob hovering over a field. Do you now feel the need to change some of the space beneath the skin or not? Would you put windows in different places, or doors? Would you change the furnishings? Will your home sound and feel different?
>
> How do you judge these skins and these spaces? What criteria do you use to measure them? Are they concrete things or abstract ideas?

Focusing on the architectural fabric of their fictional world allows writers to immerse themselves and their reader in a detailed materiality that can infuse the entire work. Umberto Eco, for example, explained the measures he took in his preparation for *The Name of the Rose*, a historical crime novel set in a medieval monastery. He needed, he said, to fully comprehend the architectural spaces he was creating, and most importantly, the navigation between them, the movement the structures allowed being as significant as the secrets they held in stasis. As well as drawing maps and studying the architectural plans of similar monasteries, he spent time calculating the number of steps in the spiral stairway and the paces between the cloister and the refectory. This research, he made clear, was not an esoteric exercise for its own sake but so that the exact requirements of the space could inform action: by knowing the number of paces his characters would need to walk a particular route, for example, he could judge how long a conversation between them could be and, in turn, how much information might be revealed.

But the conversations in this chapter have also pointed towards a more challenging and elusive element of shared practice. While the exacting process of architectural construction allowed Eco to conceive of an authentic fictional medieval monastery, the nature of the spaces the novel contains, the characters' inhabiting of these spaces and the reader's intrusion into them is not simply a process of mapping and measuring. Like the visions facilitated by the aleph, the spaces created by fiction are complex and shifty; the operation of language in defining and containing them remains obscure. Returning to the metaphor of writing fiction as entering a house that 'encloses space and makes connections between one enclosed space and another', Alice Munro emphasizes this problem of pinpointing a concrete replicable technique, resorting to the importance of feeling, however imprecise and 'indescribable', to capture what happens in the process of writing these spaces:

> So when I write a story I want to make a certain kind of structure, and I know the feeling I want to get from being inside that structure. This is the hard part of the explanation, where I have to use a word like "feeling," which is not very precise, because if I attempt to be more intellectually respectable I will have to be dishonest. "Feeling" will have to do ... I've got to make, I've got to build up, a house, a story, to fit around the indescribable "feeling" that is like the soul of the story, and which I must insist upon in a dogged, embarrassed way, as being no more definable than that.[35]

Munro's insistence on a story's 'soul' reaches towards the physical and imaginative intersection between story, time and space which this chapter has explored in discussion with architecture. While this 'soul' remains intangible, my conversations in this chapter have emphasized the importance of creative sight in going some way towards finding and expressing it, in much the same way as Borges relied on the verb to see in his attempts to express the potentiality of the aleph. Matteo Pericoli discusses the moment when 'literary structure, emotions and feelings' are translated into something visible, 'into proportions, light, darkness, solids and voids'.[36] And Gordon Grice is clear that the key is 'a question of visualisation'. It's this skill of visualization, he suggests, which architects can bring to other disciplines, especially writing; an appreciation of architectural technique can help the writer understand and manage the spaces in fiction: 'it's through the arrangement of space as much as narrative that you see things like cause, motive and characterization which are so important', he says. Form, structure and space animate ideas and characters rather than simply contain them, he points out, and at the moment when we see this animation, architecture and fiction converge.

As Gordon identifies, thinking creatively and concretely about the spaces we construct on the page enables our fiction to move beyond simply being *about* the spaces it narrates. Instead it becomes fully alive *within* them. For architects, it's this ability of fiction to animate and fully imagine space that can be valuable, to import the suggestive and fleeting, the 'ghosts' advocated by Pedro Gadanho. Emphasizing the open-ended plasticity of story and the intrinsic links between making spaces and writing them, the cultural critic and writer Carola Hilfrich has highlighted this 'humanness' that is made possible when architects interact with fiction, 'the potential choreography' which shapes and communicates spatiality: 'the potential choreography between our bodies, imagination, and the built environment … our communicative sense of spatiality – the moments where literature and architecture, words and buildings and spaces, readability and inhabitability intertwine with humans'.[37]

It seems clear to me, then, that the accidental convergence of lines that occurred in my mind's muddling of desire lines and reading between the lines anticipated a genuine and fruitful intersection between writing and architecture, and in particular in the ways in which we use and imagine space, as explored in this chapter. While we might, in the absence of clear definitions and technical blueprints, occasionally need to resort to Munro's dogged, embarrassed insistence on 'feeling', there is nonetheless, clear evidence of shared processes of conceptualization. This is exciting ground that seems to offer solid foundations for rewarding and generative collaboration. Immersed in his architectural worldbuilding for *The Name of the Rose*, Umberto Eco noted that 'our lives are full of interstices', spaces that are pregnant with possibility, which are active, peopled and productive for the writer, and physically present for the reader.[38] For the architect, this notion of interstices is also powerful, offering 'the spaces between idea and thing, where perfect correspondence is never entirely found, demanding a realm of endless negotiation and productive interpretation'.[39] In occupying and imagining these interstices, the writer and the architect create spaces for human emotions, philosophies and events to play out.

4

Plot/Medicine

Let's begin this chapter by imagining a garden. Flowers, if you prefer, or vegetables, perhaps a tree or two. It may be a beautifully tended allotment, cultivating a range of tasty produce, or it might be a wilder place, weedy and unkempt; the composition of the garden, what it contains and how it grows, might change with the seasons, or years, or fashion. But despite all these variables, the garden remains a recognizable size and shape. It supports and contains the multiplicity and simultaneity of activity happening inside it: games of football, insect lives, budding plants, dogs, rodents, barbeques, herbaceous borders, tangles of roots below and birds perching above. And perhaps most importantly, the garden is fenced or hedged, marked out from the land around it and bounded in some way, distinguished from the patchwork of other gardens. Someone has laid claim to it, even if only on the deeds lodged with the Land Registry, and in this act of laying claim, of delimiting, the garden has been assigned an identity and a purpose within the wider structured pattern of land use. It has become recognized as a plot.

This garden, this plot, helps us consider another type of plot – the series of events that come together in a story. The sense of an organized, intentional space is shared by both, and the image of the garden plot reminds us of the importance of the walls and fences, of containment: the fiction plot, too, requires limits and boundaries so that it can be encompassed within the memory of the reader, allowing her to keep track and follow the logic the writer proposes. The fiction plot, like the garden, is a place that accommodates, and allows to flourish, all manner of other things: characters live here among the weeds, metaphors and motifs twine up against the walls, actions and events define its topography. It is both a mundane assemblage of paths and stakes and markers and beds, and a place of discovery and revelation. While it is sometimes dismissed as the populist territory of the genre novel or a dull but necessary question of mechanics, at a fundamental level, plot is essential to fiction and can't be shrugged off or ignored – no matter how spectacular the flower display in the garden, a simple piece of demarcated land is required to sustain it. So in this chapter, I intend to dig around the muddy tangle of plot to look at how it underpins the writer's craft and, in particular, to make connections with some of the essential processes of medical practice. I'll be talking to doctors about their conversations with patients and looking especially at the medical history, which informs the development of a diagnosis.

Most of us are accustomed to giving accounts of our health to family and friends, colleagues, doctors, other patients; we instinctively plot our trajectory from well to sick or from sick to recovered. We attach stories to our physical experience; we create them through and with our bodies. Recognizing this process of medical storytelling, the concept of 'narrative medicine' is now well established, widely accepted as a means by which the practitioner and patient negotiate and express illness. Over thirty years ago, Kathryn Montgomery Hunter laid the groundwork for an emerging interest in an intersection between medicine and narrative in her book, *Doctors' Stories*, which brought to light the underlying importance of story in everyday medical interactions: medicine, she noted, 'is an interpretive activity' that requires physicians to develop 'a literary sense of the lives in which illness and medical care take place'.[1] Emerging as a distinct field of research by the turn of the century, the practice of narrative medicine became closely connected to humanities traditions, advocating close reading skills and teaching creative writing and literary criticism to medical practitioners. The concept might include reflective writing or the writing of stories by doctors or patients, inspired by or recounting their experiences. It explores issues of interpretation and how we apprehend meaning, emphasizing the role of the reader and how an understanding of the complexities of textuality can influence patient care. Narrative medicine embraces better listening and the importance of nuanced conversation. It's regarded as a model for empathy and reflection. The British psychiatrist,

Femi Oyebode, writes eloquently about the importance of being able to use imagination to understand others and to access their suffering: 'When you read fiction, or biography, or when you read a memoir, you're practising this capacity to understand the other, and it is also always self-reflective. You're accessing the nature of human suffering; you read to understand another ... For medicine, literature in particular can help to facilitate this capacity to imagine the other properly'.[2]

The theory and practice of narrative medicine is wide-ranging, then, and adopts a number of different literary techniques, but in this chapter I intend to focus my attention on the specifics of plot. The mechanics of plotting have received less attention in medicine than broader conceptualizations of narrative, so here I want to consider why plot, in particular, might be significant in medical interactions, exploring the processes by which medical professionals construct plot and how these processes might correspond to those of fiction writers. In my conversations, I'll be discussing how doctors understand plot and how far they are influenced by the way writers plot their work, and I'll be reflecting on what we might learn as writers from the ways in which plot is used in medical practice.

There's a long and sometimes conflicting literature examining the significance of plot in fiction. Aristotle argued that plot, 'mythos', is the most important element of storytelling: 'it is the action in it, i.e. its Fable or Plot that is the end and purpose'; his analysis of a good plot as one which presents an organic unity, free from irrelevant incident, and demonstrating a probable or necessary succession of events, has been influential.[3] In an attempt to theorize the workings of plot, structuralist critics of the mid-twentieth century defined it more closely as how the writer presents events, so dividing it from story (what happens), as we've seen in Chapter 1. Later critics challenged this separation, making an argument for plot containing both story and its ordering: Paul Ricœur, for example, argues that 'plot *makes* events *into* a story'.[4] More recently, Christopher Booker's *The Seven Basic Plots: Why We Tell Stories* (2004) provided a persuasive model for recognizing and defining different plot types, creating a framework for writing plot based on an analysis of archetypal stories. A three-act structure, adapted from storytelling to film, has also become a significant element in contemporary views of plotting: its construction of a journey from set-up to confrontation and resolution is prominent in screenplays and frequently taught on screenwriting courses. Now, developments in cognitive science and particularly in AI have changed the way in which we produce and read texts. The automatic generation of plots is one of the tasks more easily accomplished by AI software since, rather like Booker's model, it can trace and adopt the common elements found in large numbers of plots and focus on those that readers find most engaging; AI is well placed for imposing Aristotle's rules of logic and relevance.

Central to all these analyses is the idea of plot as the imposition of some kind of pattern, which helps us understand how and why events take place – this is the sense in which I'll be employing the term in this chapter. In life, any such pattern might be difficult or impossible to discern (at least until we're on our deathbed) and of course might not even exist. Unless we believe in design imposed by external forces, such as deities, then most likely our lives will appear as a collection of events held together only loosely by their belonging in some way to us and given a sense of plot only by the temporal unfolding of a lifespan. This connection of plot to time fascinated many nineteenth-century writers who explored the idea that knowledge or truth could only be understood through a sequential progress, and only over time could readers and writers understand how human life might acquire significance. This in turn led to the popularity of the bildungsroman, and what Peter Brooks identifies in *Reading for the Plot* as 'the promise of progress towards meaning'.[5] Viewed in this way, plot offers an unfolding of a hidden purpose, gradually making clear the causality of what happens so that the reader can understand not just what has taken place but also why. Fairytales are often held up as good examples of this kind of plotting, which is seen as transmitting an essential wisdom and in so doing offering a means of reasserting order over chaos, allowing the reader to speculate on strange goings-on with the assurance that things will ultimately fall into place.

In more contemporary fiction, however, there can be multiple temporalities in action (as we've seen in Chapter 1) and a sequence of events or sense of interconnectedness may remain purposely concealed, leading to a more complicated patterning and a more obscure grasp of any authoritative plot. Television crime drama, for example, commonly presents several events occurring in slightly differing time frames and with no apparent connection to each other: a political meeting takes place in the city hall at the same time as a murder is discovered in remote woodland and a plane lands at an airport in a neighboring country. But this strategy of challenging the reader/viewer to discover links – in effect, to seek out the plot – is not as new as it might appear. In an early chapter of *Bleak House* (1852–3), for example, Charles Dickens poses a series of questions with the explicit intention of linking what appear to be disparate places and people, and so provoking speculation about the plotting of what follows:

> What connexion can there be between the place in Lincolnshire, the house in town, the Mercury in powder, and the whereabout of Jo the outlaw with the broom, who had that distant ray of light upon him when he swept the churchyard-step? What connection can there have been between many people in the innumerable histories of this world who from opposite sides of great gulfs have, nevertheless, been very curiously brought together!

Dickens' questions draw attention to the importance of the reader's role in making a plot work, encouraging them to interact with the process and directly prompting them to piece together meaning in a dynamic way. Peter Brooks describes this as evoking a form of desire in the reader; one reason this approach to plotting has become more evident in recent decades is because, rather like the three-act structure, this notion of desire on the part of the viewer has become integral to plotting in film, particularly in commercial Hollywood blockbusters. In this iteration, plotting is not just about the unity and logic that Aristotle proposed, and which is a product of the writer's design, but also about exciting curiosity, emotional investment and a strong wish for a particular outcome, which switches attention from writer to reader. Here, an emphasis inevitably falls on endings, since making full sense of what has happened is only possible retrospectively, and satisfaction (or disappointment) for the reader is dependent on desire being fulfilled (or thwarted). As E. M. Forster noted, with the most successful plots, the reader:

will constantly rearrange and reconsider, seeing new clues, new chains of cause and effect, and the final sense (if the plot has been a fine one) will not be of clues and chains, but of something aesthetically compact, something which might have been shown by the novelist straight away, only if he had shown it straight away it would never have become beautiful.[6]

While making 'something aesthetically compact' and 'beautiful' in this way has sometimes been regarded as a rather prosaic fiction skill – the clumsy cousin to complex characterization or lyrical language – plotting remains an inescapable part of the writing process. (After all, the plot synopsis forms an important element of any submission to literary agents or publishers.) And Brooks suggests that, in fact, plot should be regarded as the most significant and fundamental fiction technique, 'the very organizing line, the thread of design, that makes narrative possible … the principle of interconnectedness and intention which we cannot do without in moving through the discrete elements – incidents, episodes, actions – of a narrative'.[7] Further, he makes the claim that the appreciation of plot that we bring to fiction extends beyond the page to the way in which we understand the patterns governing our lives: 'Plot … thus comes to appear one central way in which we as readers make sense, first of the text, and then, using the text as an interpretive model, of life'.[8] It's this view of plotting as a key element in both fiction and life that will provide a starting point for my conversations with medical professionals, a shared understanding that plotting is not some cumbersome device best played out in genre fiction but a dynamic, energetic activity which shapes time and place, an expression of internal energies and tensions, propulsions and resistances that is integral to the way in which we experience the world.

The ways in which the writer resolves diverse events through the complex patterning of a plot form the basis for much of the work in narrative medicine. The American doctor and literary scholar, Rita Charon, who founded the field, draws specific attention to the role of plot in enabling us to comprehend and express relationships, experiences, impulses and actions. It's in and through plot, she points out, that characters in fiction are able to 'address the unknown, to tame danger, to conquer fear, to brave, full in the face, any predicament in which a human being finds himself or herself' and it's these same qualities, she proposes, which enable patients to examine and express their medical situation.[9] Charon builds her approach to narrative medicine on the medical history, which in basic terms is the conversation a patient has with a doctor when they discuss symptoms and concerns with a view to making a diagnosis. The standard medical history, or anamnesis, consists of the doctor directing the patient to reveal specific facts about their illness, including the time course and severity of their symptoms; exacerbating and remitting factors; past medical events, including any major interventions, such as surgeries; details of family medical conditions; and social factors (which might include such things as work patterns, how much the patient drinks or whether they smoke). This leads to a physical examination and an assessment by the doctor, culminating in a treatment plan. The aim of the medical history is to guide the doctor towards a small number of possible diagnoses; the formula is routinely taught to medical students and subsequently reinforced through use in a variety of formal and informal settings that range from hospital grand rounds to discussions during everyday practice; it has remained unchanged for at least a century, featuring, for example, as a core framework in Georg Klemperer's 1898 *The Elements of Clinical Diagnosis*. Following this brief conversation, the physician then records the encounter in the records, rewriting the patient's story into a formal case history.

The process underpinning the medical history relies on the bringing together of two kinds of information: the data that informs the medical detection process – such as vital signs or evidence from the physical examination – and a narrative shaped by what the patient has said and how they've said it. Unsurprisingly, this narrative frequently follows a distinct plotting pattern expressing a change of state from health to sickness, but the specifics of it will vary with every patient, and it's these specifics that are important in piquing a physician's professional curiosity. For Charon, the role of narrative medicine is to embed into this process an additional emotional interaction, the facility for the doctor to 'be moved'; she defines narrative medicine as 'medicine practiced with the narrative competence to recognize, absorb, interpret, and be moved by the stories of illness'.[10] But as Montgomery Hunter points out, there are also complex negotiations of story at play beyond the humanizing of the experience of illness, the idiosyncrasy and uncertainty of the patient's plot sitting in tension with the diagnostic methodology of the plot imposed by the doctor. The patient thinks of their story as unique, perhaps even worthy of exceptional attention; the doctor is constantly attempting to normalize it by fitting it into a pattern (or wider plot) that they recognize:

> the patient's story straddles the lines between history and scientific investigation and as a consequence is regarded both with careful attention and with a skepticism [sic] which sometimes amounts to disdain and suspicion ... The patient is speaking of what is often quite intimate experience, drawing upon a sense of self, while the physician, however empathic, is objectively engaged in solving a problem.[11]

The comparatively recent advent of online search engines, such as Google, adds another dimension to this negotiation. The patient, having researched their complaint before the medical appointment, may well arrive with their own plot, which can act as a counter-narrative to the doctor's: the authority of the internet and the medical practitioner face off in the patient, the multiple plots tussling for primacy and the medical history forced to construct some kind of reconciliation between them.

As part of a movement towards paying attention to the nuances and instabilities of the medical history, there has been an attempt to change the language most commonly employed. Instead of a doctor 'taking' a medical history, the emphasis has shifted to doctor and patient mutually 'building' a more contextualized narrative. The importance of silences, body language, choice of words and conversational devices has also been observed. Research has examined how patients of different genders, races and cultural backgrounds experience the medical history, raising questions about authority, power and the right to speak, with a growing recognition that these questions may fundamentally alter the narrative being told and heard: 'stories change depending on the narrative situation. A 50-year-old African-American woman may not tell the same story about sexual abuse to a 20-year-old white male intern that she tells to a 60-year-old African-American female gynaecologist'.[12] The unpredictability of personal narratives, it has also been noted, is not unlike the unpredictability of disease, and so should be familiar to doctors, even if they don't always recognize the connection: 'Physicians do not expect fevers to remain unchanged. Cancer and depression do not continue in a steady state. The verb-like variations implicit in narrative would seem relatively unproblematic for physicians who deal every day with humans and diseases that unexpectedly change course'.[13]

But perhaps most relevant to our discussion, this focus on the workings of the medical history has highlighted the importance of plot. As Charon has pointed out:

> Clinical practice is consumed with emplotment. Diagnosis itself is the effort to impose a plot onto seemingly disconnected events or states of affairs. We test one diagnostic algorithm after another—and the more seasoned we get, the more automatically and underconsciously this process occurs—in the effort to categorize this set of events, in the effort to emplot it ... how many possible plots there might be hidden within a simple recitation, how many motives and antecedents might be at work, how many different points in time might be considered the "beginning" of the story.[14]

Drawing on practice from the humanities and from disciplines such as psychology and anthropology, the medical history has been addressed as a text that can be read and interpreted, its structures and assumptions revealed, its techniques analysed – and its plots understood. Through what Charon describes as 'the complex skills of imagination', the doctor becomes able to discern the plot of the patient's life and then participate within it in much the same way as the reader participates in the plots set out by the writer; 'with such knowledge', Charon notes, 'we enter others' narrative worlds and accept them – at least provisionally – as true'.[15]

It is with these 'complex skills of imagination' that I begin my first conversation. I'm speaking to Nellie Hermann, a novelist who teaches on Columbia University's seminal Narrative Medicine course and who is co-author of *Principles and Practice of Narrative Medicine*. As a writer, Nellie is fully attuned to the potential power of reading, but she explains how her student doctors need encouragement to step back from what she terms the 'heavyweight' material they're accustomed to, often seeking permission to explore new perspectives that spring from imagination and creativity. 'They think they're not creative', she says, 'but this is so wrong. So we move towards an awareness that creativity is happening in all moments and can really change their work'. She talks about the 'capacity for curiosity' which is shared by writers and doctors, and which acts as a starting point for the activities she leads on writing and reading. This curiosity, which springs from the doctors' natural desire to build knowledge, provides a point of access to the imagination. She explains how she then directs focus to the writer's craft – to habits, skills and techniques – to explore the practical ways in which the imagination might manifest, a process that includes a sharp awareness of the importance of plot.

When I ask Nellie about the role of the medical history in her work, she explains how this provides a fundamental basis to her course, which involves 'talking a lot about ideas of listening and receiving stories'. At the outset, she says, much of the discussion centres on recognizing how stories work, and what it means to share a personal story with someone else, particularly someone who might be interested in reinterpreting, or replotting, it. As patients attempt to lay out the details of their illness to a doctor, they are approaching a story that might have its roots in the past, in relationships, life choices, injuries or accidents – personal, confusing or even frightening circumstances that are unlikely to be fully understood and which the patient might be reticent about articulating. In return, the structure and language of the medical history often create a distance between practitioner and patient, so that even if the words employed by the doctor are ostensibly familiar, the new context makes them strange, meaning the patient might struggle to follow the story being constructed about them or to fashion it in a way that feels authentic to them. Nellie begins the process of untangling these multiple and sometimes antagonistic elements by helping her students better grasp the complexity of story. This, she says, requires an emphasis on alert and creative reading. 'Before we can even talk about writing, we talk about reading', she explains, outlining how this exploration of what makes a good reader can be a lengthy process and one that presents her students with completely new skills and perspectives. Doctors, she says, 'are not experienced at reading for craft', but by understanding how a symptom or a disease recounted by a patient can be read in the same way as an event happening to a fictional character, they 'come to appreciate how the detail in a close reading, and the multiple interpretations, can unlock new analyses'.

Once Nellie's students understand these connections between story and the medical history, a more focused investigation of how plotting works helps give shape and structure to what might seem like disparate bits and pieces of information supplied by the patient. Learning to pick out the contours of a plot, she says, helps bring together the fragments of language and imagery, allowing the experience to emerge in a discernible form and ultimately enabling the doctor to approach the chaotic multiplicity of the story they're being told in what she calls 'a writerly way'. The emphasis on listening skills allows this plot to run its course, she explains, drawing a direct comparison between the doctor and the reader: just as a reader has to keep faith with the writer's intention by following through the plot of a story to its end, so the doctor learns how to co-construct a more comprehensive and meaningful final story through effective listening – rather than 'spoiling the plot' by jumping in to direct what the patient is saying and in what sequence. Although, as Nellie admits, listening and reading skills don't always come naturally: many of the doctors she works with 'are definitely freaked out' by the prospect of reshaping their practice in this way.

Rita Charon positions plot at the heart of clinically effective narrative medicine:

> The better equipped clinicians are to listen for or read for a plot, the more accurately will they entertain likely diagnoses and be alert for unlikely but possible ones. To have developed methods of searching for plot or even imagining what the plot might be equips clinicians to wait, patiently, for a diagnosis to declare itself, confident that eventually the fog will rise and the contours of meaning will become clear ... a similar combination of cognitive, affective, imaginative, and characterological abilities are called into play in finding plot in narrative and making a diagnosis in unwellness.[16]

She draws attention to 'the storied shape of reality' and the ways in which 'we create meaning by weaving the fragments of life into plot'.[17] Nellie points out that, ultimately, it's difficult to prove that better understanding and mastery of writing skills makes any difference to clinical expertise – 'the connections are oblique', she says, 'how can you prove it translates in practice?' – but she is nonetheless convinced of the value of a nuanced understanding of language, an alertness to gaps and omissions, and a training in creative and critical inquiry. The focus on structure, ordering, discovery and possibility that plot particularly enables can and should have a significant core role in medicine, she suggests, as well as in other disciplines. Her work is not about using reading and writing to create a commentary or appendix to medical practice, she emphasizes, but to thoroughly embed the techniques, highlighting the equal importance and status of creative practice. 'It makes me sad', she says, 'it's shame, that we tend not to talk about how we can use our writing skills in a practical way'.

Finding the Plot

Write a fictional dialogue exchange that occurs when a patient visits their doctor to discuss something that's bothering them. Consider which questions the doctor will use to prompt information. Decide what the patient will choose to divulge and withhold about their experience. At the end of the consultation, what has been revealed, agreed or decided? Where might the story go from here?

Now the patient is telling the story of their illness to a close friend with whom they feel comfortable chatting. They are giving the same information but using different language and with a re-ordered narrative. They are emphasizing different elements of their experience. Write this new dialogue exchange. How do the friend's questions differ from the doctor's? How does this prompt different answers, and so change the plot? What has come to the fore or been set aside? Where does the story go now?

Our reading (and writing) of plot is not, of course, a uniform experience. Some books, and genres, offer more of a sense of plottedness than others; the dynamics of plotting have changed over time. The publishing of many nineteenth-century novels in several volumes or as serials brought plot to the fore, driving the reader from one installment to the next – and from one purchase to the next – by offering an expansive cast of characters all involved in their own dramas but interlinked in a complicated plot. Peter Brooks holds up Dickens' *Great Expectations* as the best example of this kind of plotting (indeed, of plotting in general) outlining how Pip, an orphan, is shown in the opening to the novel at his parents' grave, tracing his name and in search of his life, his plot. He's interrupted in his grief by the intrusion of a mysterious stranger, Abel Magwitch. This kind of unexpected arrival is a classic plot device, upsetting the status quo; in the case of *Great Expectations*, Magwitch immediately changes Pip's situation, physically and emotionally. Despite Magwitch's intervention, however, the train of events that follows directs attention away from him and towards Satis House and its inhabitants, which is quickly established as the object of desire for both Pip and the reader, a place of dreams and, of course, expectations. The plot of the novel and of Pip's life apparently centres around, and is dependent on, Miss Haversham and Estelle. But in fact, as Brooks points out, it's the 'repressed convict plot' that is shown to be the more powerful, and the real driver of the action: 'the story that Pip would tell about himself has all along been undermined and rewritten by the more complex history of unconscious desire, unavailable to the conscious subject but at work in the text'.[18] Pip, and often the reader, get the story wrong. They misunderstand and misread the plot, which is propelled throughout by Magwitch and a determinative past rather than by Miss Haversham and a romantic future.

By the first half of the twentieth century, writers like James Joyce and Virginia Woolf were attempting to expose the artifice of the nineteenth-century tradition of plotting, offering a more ironic approach that emphasized the messiness and incomprehensibility of characters' lives. Bold, sweeping plots tended to give way to more intimate experience, which was subject to fantastical turns – often the result of inner thought rather than outer event – and a conscious subversion of unifying structures. But the writer's fundamental question of plotting still remained: how do we create a coherent fictional structure from the muddle of life? This is a question I raise during my next conversation, with psychiatrist Dr Steven Hastings, who joins me from his home in rural Wales where he practises. Psychiatry, he points out, is a branch of medicine that's explicitly engaged with helping patients plot a way through such a muddle, 'establishing the key moments in a patient's life, what stands out' and particularly 'how to interpret what that person sees as significant'. But it's precisely because human experience is so complex that he's wary about the question of plotting and warns against promoting it as an easy solution, adding that he sometimes feels like pushing for a new discipline of 'unnarrative medicine' that resists the need to tie everything into a neat plot. 'People like plots', he says, 'they gravitate towards plotting', but for many of his patients, the important thing to point out is that 'most of the time things are messy, coincidental, beyond our control'. The drive for plot, he explains, is not necessarily helpful. 'Art, sculpture, writing', he says, 'are often about artifice, making things fit a pattern of some kind, making them pleasing'. He uses the example of crime writing in which the notion of plot traditionally became associated with conspiracy, the writer being encouraged (and sometimes required) to weave schemes, betrayals and red herrings to purposely misdirect and puzzle readers before offering a satisfying resolution. By contrast, he says, his role is not to apply artifice but to try to strip it away: 'my job is to take people away from the idea that everything has to fit a plot'.

As we talk, Steven expands on the potential pitfalls of applying fictional plotting to the medical history. For the writer, he says, the more neatly the elements of the story tie together, the more highly we tend to value the skill. So, with the increasing popularity of genre fiction during the twentieth century, most obviously perhaps in crime, mystery and thriller novels but also adventure, romance, horror and Westerns, recognizable plot conventions and structures became concretized, and plotting control became regarded as an important fictional technique. On screen, the influence of television drama – with a return to the serialized forms of the Victorian novel – reaffirmed the importance of tight plotting alongside the story arc of strong characterizations. But for many of his patients, Steven explains, 'the pressure to fit life into a recognisable plotting framework like a television series can be problematic'. Such explicit and pervasive fictional order can lead to a drive to connect and simplify in real life, sparking a fruitless and painful search for a plot to make sense of situations that just don't allow for it. As he points out, our lives don't follow such a structured course: 'we have to confront things beyond our control'.

As Steven explains how his work as a psychiatrist enables him to challenge this instinctive impulse to make a patient's interpretation of life events fit a plot, he returns to the role of the medical history. Because plotting is not as straightforward as it might seem, and because a personal plot can be so life-changing, a nuanced approach to the medical history is always important, he says. He outlines how in psychiatry, physical and psychiatric symptoms often overlap in a complex way, which can make it particularly difficult for a patient to fit together all the difference aspects of their illness and interpret the story they're telling. There's a lot going on in their lives, and often they are unable to see the connections, sometimes reading their situation in a completely different way to those around them. 'You want to let the patient have ownership of their story', he says, 'but often their interpretation of this story has gone awry'. So while patients might be wedded to a view of their life events which makes up a particular plot, this can easily be a distorted version that 'isn't necessarily the real story, and family and friends would fail to agree on the plot as the patient presents it'. This is where the medical history provides a way of focusing on the most significant elements of a patient's account: in the same way as a writer constructs a plot from all the possible options, leaving aside some parts of the story and emphasizing others in order to guide the reader to a particular interpretation, so it's during the medical history, Steven explains, that the doctor begins to see 'how you might make a different plot from the same events'. So at the outset, a patient might 'see themselves as the product of other, generic plots', and these generic stories 'tend only have one ending', but through the exhaustive conversation grounded in the medical history, the psychiatrist, he says, begins to make possible different story arcs, 'enabling people to write a different ending'.

As Steven points out, however, getting to an ending, or even distinguishing what might act as an ending, requires the doctor to understand how to pick out chronologies revealed by a medical history much as a reader might pick their way through the possible chronologies offered by a writer (echoing Nellie's emphasis on the doctor as reader). In the same way that, as writers, we might employ temporal change – flashback or flashforward, for example – to steer a reader's sense of a plot, so the basic chronology of the patient's plot can be subject to a series of alterations and manoeuvres that modify the original timeline. The straightforward organization of facts with which they begin their story – this happened and then illness struck, and this was the result – is reworked both in their own telling and as doctors move back and forth in search of a diagnosis, rather like fictional detectives sifting through multiple time frames of evidence in a crime story. In our conversation, Steven draws attention to the multiple temporalities of a good medical history, which, while grounded in the present, has 'present, past and future in mind at the same time'. He reminds me how doctors talk about a patient's 'presentation', that is, the way they are feeling in the present, why they have come to talk to a doctor in that moment, but he points out how much of his work is concerned with piecing together different time frames, 'what's brought them to this point from the past and what would they like to change, what might a future look like. You're never just fixated on the moment you're dealing with – you always having a temporal line in your mind'. Patients, too, he says, inevitably manipulate the chronologies of the plot they're recounting, as you might when telling any story, and their decisions can be of consequence in understanding their case. 'When you give people free rein', he says, 'the point at which they choose to start the timeline is significant'. Not only are the doctor and patient trying to work out how the past relates to the present – as the term 'medical history' implies – but they are also attempting to identify 'at what moment their life deviated from the plot they expected; how far back do we have to go to find a healthy you; when did change occur'. He suggests this echoes both the craft of the writer in looking for moments of transformation in constructing plots for their characters, and also the engagement of the reader: the plot that emerges during the medical history or consultation is about making temporal links, in the same way a reader is asked to piece together different temporalities into a coherent fiction.

In her analysis in *Doctors' Stories*, Montgomery Hunter also highlights questions of chronology, describing the physician's tentative hypotheses as a circling around clues, a 'plot of discovery' which she compares to the plots of Sherlock Holmes stories, and which results in a much more complex chronology than the patient first describes:

> the life events narrated in the patient's story and their interpretation as medical events in the case presentation thus take part in two different plots … the represented time in the medical narrative is not the lived time of

the illness but the plotted time of medical discovery ... the medical plot, the narrative organisation of the case, is shaped by the physician's quest for an understanding of the patient's illness: a diagnosis.[19]

Finally, the end of the plot is usually restoration to health, or otherwise, but closure is experienced differently by the doctor and the patient: the doctor recognizes closure in a successful diagnosis and treatment plan, the patient's plot is ongoing as they continue to live with the illness or its effects. The original plot has been reconfigured both by varying points of view and for divergent purposes, events selected and organized in quite different ways and resulting in quite different plots.

But it's not only the ending of a patient's story that might be reshaped as their plot is revisited. From the moment when a patient brings their story to a doctor – which might be regarded as the classic inciting incident that kickstarts a fictional plot – many subsequent plots are possible. The beginning remains open, subject to a series of questions and characterized by unformed and possibly conflicting hypotheses. At this point, the story resides with the patient; it is the patient who organizes the material into a plot that they recognize as authentic. But just as Pip's sense of his life plot is 'undermined and rewritten' by more complex external machinations of which he's largely unaware, so subsequently, it's the doctors who take charge of plotting, reconstructing what they've been told, testing the patient's reality against physical findings and test results, and re-telling the story in medical charts, as the subject of hospital rounds or case conferences, possibly even as the basis for publication. As Montgomery Hunter points out, 'medicine has the power not only to rewrite the patient's story of illness but also to replot its course'.[20] The patient's original sense of their plot can become at best distorted and at worst meaningless as their original story is superseded and a new set of meanings imposed. Proponents of narrative medicine would argue that by placing themselves and their interventions inside, rather than outside, the plots they construct with patients, they can better understand the key role they play in the creation and direction of this plot, and the power they wield as they requisition the plots of the patients with whom they're working.

The Plot Thins

Work with a friend or learning partner. Take turns to share a health story – either a real one, or one you've made up. Make careful notes as you listen to your partner's history of their illness. Better still, record everything they say.

Using your notes, construct a word cloud. In the largest letters and the boldest colours, write the single words used most frequently in the telling of the story (e.g. breath, leg, pain). Now work through the rest of the history, making smaller words for issues the patient raised less frequently (e.g. mum, work, internet). In the end, you should have a pictorial representation of the patient's concerns and priorities.

What is revealed by compressing the plot in this way? When you look at the word cloud, are you surprised by the emphases? Are these different from the ones you'd imagined when you first listened to the history? Are there words in the cloud that you had not considered when listening?

When doctors can recognize the process of shaping, claiming and appropriating plots, this influences their personal practice and has been shown to achieve better outcomes for patients. I've arranged to speak to Dr John Launer, founding president of the Association of Narrative Practice in Healthcare, who holds a number of senior clinical roles in general practice and family therapy as well as a first degree in English Literature. John's lifelong interest in literature and storytelling has been significant in directing his own practice; he's written about how sharing perspectives through story satisfies a basic human need and how the act of building narratives between patient and doctor may, in itself, have therapeutic value. For our conversation, he joins me from his spacious and elegant London study. As we discuss some of the differences between a clinical and a therapeutic approach, he begins by explaining how experiencing other people's stories can be a way of breaking down what he terms 'estrangement', helping us to escape from our own certainty and enabling us to envision the reality experienced by others. In particular, he says, he's interested in tracing how a patient's account might be reshaped from being 'a flow of words … merely the way that people communicate their problems' to a story with meaning, and hence a plot.

It's this process of shared reshaping, of participatory plotting, which is key, John suggests. In the traditional medical history, he says, the patient narrative is reframed by the doctor into a 'truth discourse', but he calls this 'a banal form of re-storying'. With greater narrative awareness, the doctor might, as we've seen, move towards better listening in order to construct a consensual narrative; this, John says, is 'not banal, but not very creative'. It's in therapeutic dialogue, he claims, that the therapist is able to 'move in and out in a much more responsive way', seeking a co-created story in which both parties find meaning. The medical history, he says, *is* a plotting but is limited, 'a constrained plotting'. He gives the example of a patient who complains of sudden weight loss: the patient might think this is caused by stress, the doctor considers the possibility of cancer or another serious disease. The doctor's plotting options, he points out, are constrained by the physical evidence; there's 'not much scope for co-construction'. In contrast, the therapist 'has much more wiggle room', and, importantly, is not necessarily on a quest for resolution. The therapist, he says, recognizes the significance and value of a partial plot, a story that remains unfinished and that is 'claiming to be provisional'. He makes a helpful analogy with Dickens' writing processes, in which he worked through the novels in installments with neither writer nor reader knowing what was coming next.

John's approach to narrative practice has been formalized in a framework called 'Conversations Inviting Change'. These conversations are predicated on a series of similarly alliterative concepts identified as curiosity, contexts, complexity, challenge, caution and care. When I explored these before speaking to him, I was struck by their similarity to the structure of fictional plotting. Curiosity, the Conversations tell us, is 'a focused and committed interest in where the story might go. Curiosity of this kind is not just something intellectual. It involves emotional engagement as well'. This curiosity seems to chime directly with a plot opening to a piece of fiction – provoking questions and interest about 'where the story might go' and demanding an emotional commitment from the reader.[21] Looking at the next stages of the Conversations, context and complexity, I am reminded of the ways in which plots are popularly described as 'thickening', expanding to accommodate relationships, subplots, foreshadowing and rising action. Context and complexity are described in the Conversations as 'embedded in history and geography, in lifelong personal and family experience, in gender and class relations, in interest groups and in faith communities' and offering 'potential for change'[22] These elements, then, offer clear parallels with the ways in a plot expands as a work of fiction progresses, encompassing the exploits and emotional bonds of a range of characters and addressing place, setting and social ties. The emphasis on 'potential for change' brings to mind the pivoting of plot at key turning points that incite change in the protagonists. The final concepts in the Conversations, challenge and caution, are defined by John as moments that confront and redirect a patient's story, 'that offer the potential for new and unexpected directions'. This again has clear resonance with fiction where obstacles and diversions in the plot raise the stakes and propel it along unexpected paths.

When I share my observations on these similarities with John, he's quick to recognize the correspondence, but is keen to emphasize that the concepts are 'lenses rather than steps'. The conversations, he says, require fluidity and a flexible approach in order to be effective; it's important, he points out, that they are unrestrained by a set formula – the order in which the concepts emerge and are addressed during the conversation is itself part of the narrative process. But this fluidity, too, I suggest, corresponds to the building of a plot. The way in which the writer organizes and orders events directly impacts both the character's trajectory and the reader's experience; the same story might be plotted in several different ways, and each iteration would create different emphases and outcomes. John agrees. 'Re-ordering changes meaning', he says, suggesting that both writers and readers are particularly, and naturally, sensitive to slight shifts in plotting that alter the way a story is understood. He echoes Steven Hastings in reminding me that this alertness to 'telling the story in a different way' is key for doctors, too, 'not simply because it will lead to better treatment but because it will *be* better treatment'.[23]

John's claim that plotting a shared story of illness can help achieve better medical outcomes is supported by research that suggests that patients who are encouraged to share their perspective and articulate their stories have been shown to respond better and more successfully to treatment, in both medical and therapeutic settings, especially when their account is interpreted 'so as to form a coherent plot'.[24] On this basis, narrative medicine has become recognized as an important tool for building patient–doctor relationships, informing decision-making and co-ordinating care. Nonetheless, the skills are still not widely taught, more often regarded as an add-on to basic training in communication or something that can just be 'picked up' in the course of everyday practice. The integration of narrative medicine into medical settings has also faced barriers, most obviously the need to extend the time of consultations to fully allow for the co-construction of stories. Some clinicians raise concerns, too, about eliding an appropriate professional distance between doctor and patient, or about the emotional toll of fully engaging with patient stories.[25] In some cases, the concept of narrative medicine is met with clear hostility because of the lack of focus on scientific method and the difficulty (as Nellie Hermann discussed earlier) of proving efficacy, or because patients would prefer a less intrusive interaction with their doctor.[26]

Despite such reservations about introducing narrative methods more widely into medical practice, however, the connections between writing fictional lives and treating real-life illness cannot be dismissed. In particular, the fundamental awareness that all stories are constructed by creating some kind of plot, which inevitably proves critical to the way they're understood, brings our experiences and skills as writers to the heart of medical and therapeutic conversations. One of the graduates of the Narrative Medicine program at Columbia University, Indu Voruganti – now a radiation oncologist – explains how learning creative writing skills 'exercised a unique part of my brain that seemed to offer a different lens [with which] to view health care', giving her both narrative competence and a space to reflect. She emphasizes the value of storytelling not only as a patient–practitioner interaction but also among medical peers, offering a tool for navigating the challenges of intense work and 'a safe space to talk about the tragedy we're witnessing'.[27] In the anatomy of these stories, plot provides the skeletal framework, largely concealed but essential, allowing medical practitioners to structure and support intimate experience in the same way it enables design and meaning in fiction.

During our conversation, John Launer sounds a note of caution. Plotting narratives in real life, rather than in fiction, can challenge a patient's natural reticence or inarticulateness; some patients might be discomforted or overwhelmed by being asked to narrate experience, or feel disempowered in the exchange with a professional. John emphasizes that 'disease, disability, deprivation and death are not "just stories" … they each rest on a bedrock of incontestable reality'. Therapists and doctors are handling real lives and real distress; as he notes, 'professionals who get carried away by narrative ideas to the point where they forget this are not safe'.[28] But while clinical and creative practice necessarily and rightly diverge in final purpose and application, it has become clear that a nuanced understanding of how plotting works can be usefully shared by the writer and the doctor. And as Steven Hastings reminds me, it's not just a case of applying writing techniques to medicine; writers in turn can learn from looking at what is revealed by the medical history and consultation. 'People gravitate towards plotting', he says, 'so writers need to understand that this need for agency, for plot, is a fundamentally human thing. We have a basic human desire for events to make sense. So if as a writer you don't deliver on plot, the reader ends up being confused, frustrated, alienated'. Paying attention to plot is about more than just creating a pleasing order, he points out: 'It's about trying to demonstrate that our lives have meaning'.

5

Point of View/Law

Let's begin with the famous rabbit–duck illusion, which dates back to the nineteenth century, an apparently simple black-and-white drawing in which some people see a rabbit and some a duck. First used by the American psychologist, Joseph Jastrow, the illusion is aimed at demonstrating how perception is dependent not only on what our eyes tell us but also on what our brain does with this information, and how it draws on context to make sense of it. Our reaction to the ambiguity of the drawing highlights how we strive to make meaning from the things we see by filtering them through a particular perspective – and how the point of view we adopt can radically alter these meanings.

The duck–rabbit illusion is just one illustration of an apparently innate need to find an authoritative perspective that safely delivers meaning. In fiction, too, readers (and writers) grapple with the multiple possibilities of a story, and the various perspectives on offer can throw up a similar ambiguity. The relationship between point of view (the narrative voice evident in the story, or who is speaking) and focalization (the perspective or eyes through which we view the story, or who is seeing) can create an interplay of suggestion and meaning that brings the fiction to life for the reader but which can also disconcert and unsettle.[1] Just as in Jastrow's illusion, switching from one character's point of view to another's in a work of fiction similarly allows the writer to challenge initial perceptions and exploit context to present material in a new light. As the story switches from rabbit to duck, the reader is forced to reconsider what is being presented as 'truth'. Gillian Flynn, for example, swaps between the points of view of Nick and Amy Dunne in her 2012 thriller, *Gone Girl*. Both narrate the novel, and each time the point of view shifts from one to the other, the reader is asked to reconsider what they thought they knew about the couple's relationship and Amy's disappearance. As each character gives their account, the evidence appears to change, and the reader's sense of what is true is challenged.

First-person narrators like the Dunnes can add complexity to a story with the notorious unreliability of their point of view and their tendency to withhold information, controlling the reader's access to key details and engineering a particular response to the material – demanding, in effect, that the reader perceives a duck when all along the truth is rabbit-shaped. But this intentional ambiguity or uncertainty is not confined to first-person accounts. The limited or close third-person point of view, in which the writer presents the story, or elements of it, from the point of view of a single protagonist, can be similarly slippery. Here, the narrator ceases to describe a character's worldview from outside but steps inside it, fully inhabiting it so that they can present it without intervening comment. The device is often used in conjunction with free indirect discourse to lure the reader entirely into the character's thoughts and further reduce narratorial distance. Free indirect discourse – essentially, a phrase that describes the internal speech going on inside a character's head – usually lacks the 'she said' or 'he thought' tags, which help the reader identify movement from narrator to character so that the distinction between narratorial voice and a character's thoughts becomes blurred. This places an onus on the reader to identify shifts in point of view and work out through whose eyes we're being shown the action. Sometimes the transitions from narrator to character can occur so discreetly that the reader might not be sure whether a statement belongs to the author, the narrator or the character.

With its intimacy and immediacy, such a technique might appear contemporary, but it is in fact the mainstay of much nineteenth-century literature. In Anthony Trollope's *Barchester Towers* (1857), for example, the untrustworthy and ambitious chaplain, the Reverend Obadiah Slope, sets his sights on winning his power battle with the bishop's wife. Trollope lets us into Slope's plans in a passage that brings the narration directly into Slope's head:

Mr Slope, however, flattered himself that he could outmanoeuvre the lady. She must live much in London, while he would always be on the spot. She would necessarily remain ignorant of much, while he would know everything belonging to the diocese. At first, doubtless, he must flatter and cajole, perhaps yield, in some things, but he did not doubt of ultimate triumph. If all other means failed, he could join the bishop against his wife …

Free indirect speech, as here, usually retains the idiom of the speaker – exclamations, questions, dialect – within the flow of the narrative. In this case, since Slope's language and speech pattern is indicative of an education and class very similar to Trollope's, the movement between writer, narrator and character are subtle, presenting the reader with a seamless drift from one to the other and what Bakhtin identifies as an 'erasure of boundaries' between author and character.[2] Nonetheless, words and phrases such as 'doubtless' and 'If all other means failed' suggest to the reader that we are being thrust directly into Slope's machinations.

Published in the same year as *Barchester Towers*, Gustave Flaubert's *Madame Bovary* showcases a more forthright use of the close third-person technique, where internalized questions and exclamations more clearly mark the transition into a character's inner life. Flaubert's use of shifting points of view characterized his writing; his passages of free indirect style often drew attention to these modulations in perspective and voice, prompting an engagement with challenging social, cultural or political contexts and creating what has been called 'an uneasy and discomforting world'.[3] At one point, for example, we witness Emma Bovary sitting on a bench reflecting on her tangled relationships, and it becomes clear to the reader that a debate is raging in her mind:

> Whence did this insufficiency of life come from, this instantaneous decay of the things on which she relied? … if there were somewhere a being, strong and handsome, a valiant nature, filled both with exaltation and refined sophistication, the heart of a poet in the figure of an angel, a lyre with brazen cords, throbbing elegiac epithalamia up to the heavens, why then should she not chance to find him? Oh! What an impossibility!

Here, as in similar passages throughout the novel, the objective viewpoint of an omniscient narrator is explicitly set aside in an approach that transformed the understanding of what realist fiction might look like, exciting and unsettling readers and worrying the French government with its openly transgressive techniques. Following the publication of *Madame Bovary* in 1857, Flaubert was put on trial for obscenity, charged with committing 'an outrage to public morality and religion'. Although he was acquitted, the trial highlighted how the intensity and intimacy of the close third-person point of view, accompanied by free indirect discourse, foregrounded irony and created moral ambiguity. The invitation for the reader to share Emma Bovary's perspective, presenting reality as it appeared to her (and other characters) rather than filtering it through the eyes of a more objective narrator, appeared to enrage the prosecutors more than the subject matter of adultery. The technique meant that there was little room for judgement of Emma's actions by an omniscient narrator, leaving the reader to decide for himself what a correct appraisal of her situation should be. According to Roy Pascal's examination of the use of free indirect speech in the nineteenth-century novel, Flaubert's intention was not only 'to render the author invisible' but to provide a challenge to 'the prevailing conception of an author's duty' to provide moral judgement.[4] This explicit rejection of the writer's obligation to guide readers' responses seemed to baffle and enrage the prosecutor in court, Ernest Pinard, who sought in vain for a character or authorial intervention within the novel that would offer a stable, reliable position from which to denounce Emma: 'who can condemn this woman in the book?' he blustered. 'Nobody. Such is the conclusion. There is not in the book a character who can condemn her ... Would you condemn her in the name of the author's conscience? I do not know what the author's conscience thinks'.[5]

Pinard's quest for an unequivocal truth that would stand up in court, and his floundering in the face of intimate literary points of view, forms the starting point for this chapter. I want to explore how the multiple perspectives evident in a criminal trial – those of the victim and accused, the witnesses, opposing counsels, the jury and judge – can be considered in relation to the writer's use of point of view and shift of perspective in fiction. I'll be exploring how a courtroom juggles the numerous points of view that contribute to the proceedings and considering how the manipulation of point of view might impact a case. In my conversations, I'm keen to discover how far the implications of changing points of view are made explicit in court, what happens when courtroom accounts are told from multiple perspectives and what might be at stake from effective courtroom use of this fictional mainstay. Does it matter through whose eyes we witness legal evidence? And at what point does the craft of the writer and the rhetoric of legal counsel converge?

Like the medical history we examined in the previous chapter, the production of a case for and in a criminal court relies on the coherent construction of an authoritative (or at least, partially authoritative) narrative, in the form of both written legal documents and spoken courtroom discourse. Like the medical history, the narrative in a legal case frequently emerges in fragments; the lawyer, like the doctor, is charged with piecing together a story from the disparate elements tendered to them. The trial formalizes this narrative within a framework (a plot?) which foregrounds different voices in turn and presents multiple, often conflicting, perspectives, interlacing and overlapping them in the search for one that might be considered the most convincing and dominant. This search for a single accurate and reliable story is simultaneously disrupted, however, by the multiple voices and audiences that further embed the disjointed and sometimes jumbled nature of the narrative. As witnesses give evidence and are cross examined, the story diverts, doubles back; the opposing legal team, the jury and the judge all approach their role as listener from a different perspective. It is not until the very end of the trial, in the closing statements and ultimately the judgement, that the plot is finally shaped into a form that is considered worthy of conclusion.

The multivocal nature of the narrative in court, the mutating timelines and viewpoints, and the advocate's role both identifying with, and distancing from, a client's story, all point to similarities with fiction, particularly the complexities of the novel form where many situations, chronologies and subplots are marshalled by a narrator who might at different moments inhabit the characters' world or choose to remain distant. In his examination of the processes in court, Chris Heffer notes that 'stories are thus natural vehicles for presenting the patchwork' of testimonies. He traces the storytelling mode of argument back to the Athenian courts of the fourth century BCE, presenting the trial as a 'fictive trialogue between prosecution, defense and judge/jury'.[6] This highlighting of a fictive interaction is helpful to our discussion, but in modern legal practice, the sense of story is not always clearly evident. As Heffer suggests, 'the legally circumscribed, narrationally constrained, structurally fragmented and verificatory nature of trial discourse … militates against viewing it in narrative terms', while others point out that the suggestion of a storytelling approach can be unwelcome or remain determinedly unacknowledged.[7] Andrew Bricker reminds us in his analysis of judicial and case law narrative, for example, that 'storytelling might be everywhere, but it is … forever and perilously on the margins of legitimacy'.[8] The suggestion that legal practice might borrow from, or engage with, storytelling is met with antagonism by many within the profession; the idea that legal narrative might draw on fictional practice occupies a precarious position at the limits of acceptability.

I raise this issue of legitimacy with Supardi Supardi, a linguistic specialist in the Law Department at the University of Jember in Indonesia.[9] He's in no doubt that storytelling techniques play a significant role in a court of law whether they are recognized or not, going as far as to claim that the most consequential element of courtroom practice 'is in the story'. As we talk, he frequently returns to the idea of a lawyer's 'crafting' of language, with a repeated emphasis on linguistic dexterity, which links directly to the writing of fiction. The narratives heard in the courtroom, he suggests, are not just about communication, but more potently about a sophisticated 'crafting of a persuasive case dependent not on who says what to whom, but how'. Expanding on the importance of this 'how', he highlights the contribution of fiction techniques like structure and rhetoric, but also metaphor, poetic language and even rhyme, all of which can be employed, he explains, to create impact at key moments in a courtroom in the same way as they might be designed to arrest or startle the reader in a story. When I ask him about how point of view specifically contributes to this process, he returns to the problem of persuasion, suggesting that the careful application of point of view is fundamental to 'the lawyer's duty to persuade the jury' just as it is critical in the writer's efforts to persuade the reader: 'the lawyer must be able to persuade', he says, 'and the mastery of point of view is crucial to this skill'.

There is a significant body of research that examines how rhetoric is employed in legal discourse to enable control and persuasion, and how the language and structure of courtroom narratives can produce or legitimize power relations. The influence of emotive language has also been widely noted, particularly in the way in which it's used to present evidence to a jury. The psychology and tactics of narrative persuasion, too, are well studied, not least in their impact in a court of law, drawing attention to the importance of storytelling and metaphor. This is not the focus of the discussion here. But persuasion and point of view are closely connected: at the most basic level, the existence of a court case is predicated on persuading others of a particular point of view; the defendant wants the jury to believe their account. Other characters also have key roles to play in this drama of persuasion, not only accuser and defendant, but also their legal teams, the jury and the judge all bring their individual experience, knowledge, background and preconceptions to bear on the facts presented; the facts themselves are reconfigured numerous times as opposing points of view seek to make sense of them in a particular way, with the aim of incorporating them into a final, persuasive argument. Unlike a piece of fiction, a lawsuit has no predetermined ending – a jury and/or judge create their own resolution depending on the 'truth' that seems most likely or appropriate. Inevitably, then, persuading the members of the court to accept a particular point of view becomes influential in shaping this outcome. Further, because of the fragmentation of discourse in the adversarial trial – rather than despite it – point of view becomes particularly significant. If there were a single agreed narrative being heard in court then the 'how' that Supardi highlights would not be of much consequence, but the very nature of the fractured, multivocal narrative exchange necessarily brings point of view to the fore as we try to pick a way through what's being argued. When I put this point to Supardi, he nods in agreement. 'Bringing other courtroom players into the influence of your point of view is part of drawing a meaningful thread through the different versions of fact', he says.

In common law legal systems, such as those practiced in the UK and the United States, the opening statements of a trial usually lay the foundations for the contesting stories to be rolled out in installments in court over the coming days or weeks. They provide the first opportunity for each counsel to appeal to the jury's emotions and to employ a strategic point of view in order to establish sympathy and present the evidence through a particular lens. Each legal counsel acts in turn as narrator; both sides get to outline their perspective and attempt to establish its primacy. Establishing a convincing and persuasive point of view at this point can be critical to the eventual outcome of the trial: despite jurors being asked to wait until all evidence has been heard before reaching an opinion on a case, approximately 30 to 50 per cent of those taking part in mock trials report that they decide on a defendant's guilt based on what they hear during the opening statement.[10] Rather like readers scanning the first few pages of a novel deciding whether to read further, this is an important moment in terms of shaping how the various stories presented during trial will be perceived as it progresses.

In our conversation, Supardi notes the particular role of point of view at this moment, calling it the 'prime strategic consideration' that 'underpins the perception and understanding of events' to be examined in court. He draws attention to the difference between the Common Law system practiced in the UK and the United States, and his home system in Indonesia, which, as a mixed regime of civil and religious law, precludes the tradition of the opening statement and where cases are heard without a jury. It's for this reason that he has focused his research on Anglo-Saxon cases. The combination of a jury trial with a lengthy opportunity for each lawyer to present their case lends a particular significance to linguistic strategies, he says, since it foregrounds the importance of point of view in 'the lawyer's first and ultimate duty to persuade the jury'. As he points out, the stakes are high. It is the use of effective language, including sophisticated shifts in point of view, which can 'grab' the story into the hands of one side or the other, convincing the decision-makers that a particular narrative is true and ultimately 'laying the foundations for a case win'.

Analysis of historic court cases supports Supardi's assessment of the importance of the opening statement, and skillful management of point of view within it, in shaping a jury's response and creating the illusion of shared perspectives between the legal team and the listeners in the courtroom.[11] Commonly, at this point, counsel on both sides adopt a first-person narration, at least in part, setting aside the objectivity of the third person to establish relationships through a series of greetings, requests and apologies: 'Could you give me leave now to observe'; 'I have the honor to attend you as Council for this prosecution'; 'I am sorry to call back to your recollection'; 'I forgot to mention'. The effect, of course, is to humanize and personalize what might appear to be the dry facts of the case, but more significantly, this first-person address also embeds the lawyers thoroughly into the narrative they're presenting, allowing them to lay claim to the story being told. They are here, at the first opportunity, asserting their function as primary storyteller rather than simply marshal or summarizer; they are making the narrative appear as their own, and hence laying claim to the right to present it as 'truth'. *Chambers Student*, aimed at those studying law or aiming to join the bar, noted how a barrister at London's Old Bailey in a case in 2017 used the intimacy of a first-person point of view to close the gap between herself (or the character she was presenting in court) and the jurors, so drawing the jury 'ever closer into the fold' of her perspective.[12]

This impulse to lure the jury 'ever closer into the fold' can be seen even more distinctly in moments when the first-person singular 'I' is swapped for the plural form of 'we'. When this 'we' form is embedded into lengthy statements by counsel, the distance between advocate and jury is reduced still further, the narrator apparently fully aligned with the listener to create an explicitly shared point of view. Commonly, the 'we' form is employed only briefly, in short comments or asides, such as 'we can see', 'we are bound' or 'we might expect', but in these moments counsel appears to be narrating the story on the jury's behalf, implying that they share the same knowledge and experience – and the same view of the case being heard. This plural form is used much less frequently than the singular but is striking in the way it implicates jury members so thoroughly in the narrator's point of view.

What is perhaps most surprising in the analysis of courtroom language strategies, however, is the frequency with which the second-person point of view is employed, not just in addressing or posing direct questions to witnesses (which may be expected) but also, and more markedly, in interactions with the jury, especially during opening and closing statements. As writers, we rarely use this point of view extensively in fiction: Shehan Karunatilaka's 2022 novel, *The Seven Moons of Maali Almeida*, is noteworthy in its prolonged use as a means of capturing 'your self split into the you and the I, and then into the many yous and the infinite Is that you have been before and will be again'.[13] In court, however, it is not uncommon for counsel to adopt the second-person point of view. The report in *Chambers Student,* for example, detailed how both prosecution and defence switched to the second person during the critical, and potentially emotive, statements that summed up their cases at the conclusion of the trial. The prosecution turned to the jury to ask, *'But what would you do if you were a 15-year-old? Scared, in a police station, accused of murder? Would you listen to your solicitor who advised you to say "no comment" or ignore that advice?'* Similarly, the defence barrister gestured to the public gallery before asking: *'What if you were up there? A relative of the defendant? Wouldn't you want the jury to abide by the same standard of fairness that you are being asked to follow here?'* These emphatic switches in point of view, along with the body language of incorporation and inclusion and the drip-feeding of statements such as 'if you suppose', and 'you see too', effectively foreground the jury members as active participants in the story being constructed: *Chambers Barrister* noted how the tactic brought the jury into direct contact with the most serious implications of the case, eliciting 'concerned, conflicted looks on the jurors' faces'.[14] The use of direct second-person address casts each jury member as a character within the narrative frame rather than an observer outside it, highlighting their own status in the story and making them fully complicit as participant. Switching to the second person, counsel demands that jurors experience the courtroom narrative as their own.

In addition to the emotional impact of this strategy, the use of the second-person point of view places the barrister directly into a juror's thoughts, so emphasizing the elision of distance between speaker and listener and (as with the use of the 'we' form) indicating that their perspectives on the facts coincide. Research has shown that most jurors have a natural tendency to align with one of the parties involved in a trial and that when a case features missing or ambiguous information, they may rely on their own private knowledge to fill the gaps in the narrative to reinforce this alignment, just as the reader will inevitably bring their life experiences and interpretations to bear on gaps left by the fiction writer. This construction of a partly, even if unconsciously, fictionalized story by a juror can lead to different verdicts depending on whose point of view appears the most compelling.[15] In this context, counsels' attempt to manipulate sympathy by endorsing and appropriating the 'you' of the juror can be seen as a powerful advocacy weapon.

Speaking on the long-running BBC radio program *Desert Island Discs*, Michael Mansfield KC explained how his professional practice relied on seeing things from his client's perspective – on adopting and narrating the point of view of another character in the courtroom drama: 'The only way I really wanted to do the job was to get inside the shell and the shoes of the person or persons I'm representing. You have to live their lives in order to communicate their feelings and understand how they've got into the position they're in'.[16] Despite the significant implications of such a statement, there is very little published research on how getting 'inside the shell' of clients – seeing a case from their point of view – might affect the narrative presented in court and the response of a judge or jury. I raise this with Keith Belzer, a criminal defense attorney in Wisconsin who also teaches at the US National Criminal Defense College. Keith fills the screen, spilling beyond the laptop window as he leans forward, a mass of greying hair and a quick warm smile. Much of his work is about getting lawyers to understand the power of shifting point of view and the value of working from 'inside the shell'. Standing up in court, he explains, most lawyers are 'always wanting to be themselves instead of really trying to understand where the person is coming from'. With a background as a theatre manager and actor, he makes comparisons with immersive acting techniques, such as those famously advocated by Konstantin Stanislavski; without fully inhabiting the other's point of view in a similar way, he says, lawyers simply 'lose sight of the person'.

As we talk further, Keith describes a case in which he tested the impact of explicit manipulation of point of view. He was defending a vulnerable client, he explains, who had been locked up in isolation for sixty-seven days in a tiny cell called 'the hole' because the jail did not want to pay for the mental health support or medication that would be required if he was housed in the regular prison wing. In focus groups arranged before the trial, most people had said that this 'didn't seem like much', which presented Keith with what he saw as the key problem in the case: 'how to put the jury in the other's shoes?' His solution was to build a replica of 'the hole' in the courtroom and to ask his client to testify for part of the time from inside it. Going a step further, Keith employed the second-person point of view, in the present tense, to drive home the reality of the experience, prompting the client and jury with questions such as 'what are you seeing now?' 'why do you think you are here?' The effect, he says, was transformational. For fifteen minutes, the jury were 'really right there, right now', peering into the cell so intently that 'it seemed as if they weren't breathing'. The evidence became 'emotionally compelling, much more visceral', revealing what he terms 'a deeper truth than the apparent facts'. Engineering a way for the jury to fully experience, and so understand, the client's experience, and to inhabit the 'shell' of their point of view, was crucial to the wider presentation (and success) of his human rights case.

I'll return to my conversation with Keith later in the chapter, but I've arranged for now to talk to Jeanine Skorinko, Professor of Psychology at Worcester Polytechnic Institute in the United States, who has examined this process of what she terms 'perspective taking' in court, and the language that characterizes it. Jeanine's work aims to understand the psychological processes at work in a courtroom in order to unpick jurors' biases, both internal (preconceptions or prejudices) and external (such as those generated by pretrial publicity). Her research backs up the approach Keith espouses, exploring how seeing the evidence through the eyes of a particular character in the legal drama can impact a juror's decision-making, in the same way as a reader's impression of a story will be shaped by the perspective, or focalization, which the writer chooses. This contriving of perspective is rarely effected through such a dramatic reconstruction as Keith describes, but even in more standard cases, Jeanine explains, a juror adopting the defendant's perspective is likely to attach less blame to them, perhaps because of increased empathy. In contrast, a juror won over to the perspective of a victim will increase blame of the defendant. A skilfully written story will synthesize point of view and perspective to bring readers close or enforce distance, to allow access to a character's thoughts and feelings or to create secrecy and mystery, so I'm interested in the outcomes of Jeanine's research, which highlight a similar interaction in the courtroom, showing how the choice of a particular point of view leads on to the powerful manipulation of perspective, in turn impacting on the outcome of a trial.

As we talk further, Jeanine outlines a series of four experiments in which mock juries were asked to consider a case of hit and run.[17] In the first experiment, in addition to full information on the events leading to the death of a young boy, the jurors were given a fictional defence attorney's closing statement: 'Ladies and Gentlemen of the Jury, I want you to imagine how you would feel if you were in my client's shoes ... how would you feel if you were wrongly accused of a crime ....How would you feel if you were put in jail because a family needed someone to blame for the death of their loved one?' Notable for its use of second-person point of view, this explicit appeal to the jurors to stand in the 'client's shoes' and imagine themselves in the character of the defendant directly recalls Michael Mansfield's approach and, Jeanine explains, had a clear impact. Drawing the jurors into the narrative in this way occasioned 'less perceived culpability ... seeing the defendant as less guilty and less likely to commit a similar crime in the future'. Switching point of view by conspicuously employing the 'you' pronoun in this way can, she confirms, be a compelling tactic because it encourages jurors to 'draw on parts of the self' in their assessment of the defendant's character and actions.

Tweaking the timing and amount of information given to the mock jurors in the following three experiments, Jeanine's research found that even subtle manipulation of jurors' perspectives could steer feelings of empathy, influencing their perceptions of culpability and guilt, and hence the outcome of a case. Changing from the defence to the prosecuting attorney in experiment three, the facts were presented from a new perspective, but again articulated in the second person: 'how would you feel if one night you were minding your own business, walking down a main, well-lit street ... and suddenly out of the blue you were struck down by a car? How would you feel helpless on the ground?' The language and structure of the speech is very much the same as in the first experiment, but simply switching from the defendant's to the victim's perspective – changing the eyes through which the story was viewed – made the jurors more likely to convict the defendant, aligning themselves with 'the victim's desire to view the defendant as more responsible for the crime'. By contrast, the final experiment moved back to the defence team, with a simple appeal to the jurors for leniency and 'to be kind and considerate'. Even these few words were shown to be enough to engage the jurors with the defendant's perspective, leading to a lower perception of guilt.

The aim of Jeanine's research project was to understand the influences at work in court so as to be able to better predict how they might take effect. Defence attorneys like Keith, she says, tend to be convinced that it's beneficial to their case when jurors are encouraged to take a defendant's point of view. Her work aimed to provide evidence for this assumption but discovered that the link between point of view and case outcome 'was not a simple equation'. She describes the ways in which changing perspectives come into play in a criminal court as 'precarious' and emphasizes that while encouraging jurors to step into the shoes of the defendant can help them better appreciate contributing emotional, social and psychological factors, 'the research is mixed; the outcome is not guaranteed'. Such a strategy may even, she says, have a 'backfiring effect', especially by reinforcing stereotypes: 'don't underestimate how hard it can be to take someone else's perspective'. Despite this warning, what is evident from our discussion is the formidable role point of view can play in courtroom dynamics, and the significant implications of using it as a courtroom tactic. It is, she claims, 'like a weapon ... point it towards the target where it will do most good'.[18] Echoing Keith's experience with a breathless jury, 'point of view is powerful', she emphasizes; 'It can play a huge role, especially in accessing higher emotion'.

As we've begun to explore, a courtroom is a place of multiple layered points of view and perspectives. Although we've examined the use of first and second person, it remains true that most elements of a legal narrative are expressed from a third-person point of view. In documents and proceedings, the prosecution is formerly referred to as an administrative and faceless institution, such as 'The Crown' or 'The State'; the presiding judge in a case may refer to themselves in the third person in statements such as 'this court finds' or 'this court has read the briefs'; they may occasionally also use the majestic and impersonal plural 'we' form generally employed by sovereigns and diplomacy to assert distance and power (and used to quite different effect than the plural first-person already examined). As with the omniscient narrator in a piece of fiction, these strategies appear to enforce the point of view of an objective, neutral observer representing a body of institutional knowledge and upholding the authority of the law, the type of reliable narrator Ernest Pinard was searching for so desperately in the *Madame Bovary* case.

When counsel adopts the third-person construction to present evidence, however, choosing phrases such as 'my client confirms' or 'the witness states' or 'the defendant maintains', we begin to see how the implications of third-person point of view might be more complicated. While witnesses for both sides employ the first person when giving their evidence, offering a new voice in the construction of the story and inviting the jury to take account of new thoughts and feelings brought to bear on the evidence, the third-person reiteration of the same story by legal teams rapidly remoulds it. Here, I suggest, counsel is inhabiting the third-person point of view in a similar way to a close third-person narration in fiction, through a process that Roy Pascal describes as a dual voice. This occurs, Pascal explains, when the narrator 'places him/herself, when reporting the words or thoughts of a character, directly into the experiential field of the character and adopts the latter's perspective in regard to both time and place'.[19] Adopting this dual voice, counsel is simultaneously identifying with, and distancing themselves from, the witness's story. As they shape and articulate the narrative, they are inhabiting the 'experiential field' of the witness, the time and place of the testimony, and the witness's perspective. In the retelling of the witness's story, however, those in the courtroom – and the lawyer herself – are inevitably aware of an intrinsic professional independence and detachment, signalled in the formality of language and costume, which means that the inhabiting of the other point of view is destined to remain partial and even performative.[20]

Analysing this manipulation of point of view in court, American essayist and cultural critic, Elaine Scarry, makes a comparison with medical patients, which resonates with our discussion in the previous chapter. Both patients and criminal defendants, she suggests, are prohibited or discouraged from presenting their own stories, being 'often perceived as people incapable of giving a first-person report; they are unreliable narrators whose stories should be gotten away from, or around, as quickly as possible'.[21] By reframing testimony – for example: 'the witness concedes she never actually saw the defendant in the park' – the trial lawyer steps into the place of these unreliable narrators, chaperoning the statement to provide what appears to be a more stable and authoritative account of the evidence. Chris Heffer notes that this relationship between lawyer and witness positions the witness 'effectively like an internal narrator to a novelist', a simultaneous and potentially distracting voice that the lawyer has to work hard to control: 'if witnesses were allowed to tell their own stories freely, the case would lose focus and decision-makers lose concentration and focus', he claims.[22] In her analysis of US courtroom language, Gail Stygall similarly highlights how 'the original narrative – compelling, emotional, and disordered – must be transformed into legally acceptable discourse in order to be prosecutable'.[23] Keith Belzer, too, points out during our conversation that 'where you grow up' has a significant impact on your ability to express your experience as a dependable witness narrative, meaning that the legal team undertakes an important role in 'giving you those tools' to construct a legible, coherent story.

Even putting aside questions of power and right-to-speak that these statements raise, this marshalling of the witness story on the part of the legal team is not as straightforward as they might suggest. From our examination of the close third-person point of view in fiction, we recognize that the assumption of the third-person point of view to sidestep the unreliable narrator and produce a dependably consistent story might not actually generate the incontrovertible narrative of which the court is in search. In the reframing of the first-person narrative, the partial, unpredictable and subversive nature of the first-person account is only superficially circumvented, the additional third-person narratorial layer creating new gaps and interpretations. In the close third-person point of view of fiction, the capricious 'I' is replaced by the more neutral 'she' or 'he' – just as the lawyer steps in to substitute for the witness – but the writer's continued control of the narration inevitably creates space for irony and inconsistency. The reader is prompted to rummage in the interstices between what the narrator says and what is known of the character, between what is revealed by stepping into the character's point of view and what is left out.

In court, then, although counsel appears to be offering a stable and trustworthy point of view, inevitably cracks appear as facts are rearranged and evidence organized on behalf of clients and witnesses. If writers use the close third-person point of view to create irony and inconsistency, what does this mean when a similar approach is employed in a courtroom, where the aim is to achieve an agreed truth? As we've seen with *Madame Bovary*, a close third-person narrative is often intended to reflect moral uncertainty; in its non-hierarchical approach, which gives the same weight to characters' thoughts and voices as to the narrator's, it requires readers to participate in the construction of the text and make judgements about characters' reasoning and intention through an interpretative act that fills the gaps and synthesizes knowledge glimpsed in the fragments of information revealed. This sense of a fractured, multivocal patchwork of stories – equally unreliable as the shifty first-person narrator – reflects the experience in court in which scraps of evidence and understanding emerge from a series of witnesses, their first-person testimonies counterpointed by the close third-person re-telling orchestrated by the lawyer. No single viewpoint is permitted to stand for long in a process of interrogation and cross-examination. The ostensible stability and authority established in the determined imposition of a third-person perspective proves illusory.

To look more closely at how changing points of view and the manipulation of perspective can elicit incongruity, uncertainty and ambiguity, I'm turning to the work of Toni Morrison, and in particular to her 1987 novel, *Beloved*, which employs the technique to impressive effect. This is a work that begins with the detached appraising eye of an omniscient narrator offering a brief, dispassionate summary of the family and house, which are to be at the heart of the story, recalling perhaps the initial synopsis offered by a legal team in an opening statement: '124 was spiteful. Full of a baby's venom. The women in the house knew it and so did the children. For years, each put up with the spite in his own way, but by 1873 Sethe and her daughter Denver were its only victims'.[24] Characters are mostly nameless – 'the women', 'the children' – and the narrator positions herself as the authentic chronicler of 'the gray and white house on Bluestone Road' just as legal counsel aims to establish themselves in court as a similarly trustworthy source of information. It's not long, however, before this semblance of narrative order in *Beloved* succumbs to a livelier, more unsettling and more elusive mode of storytelling as the narration slides into the characters' discourse. As the opening chapter progresses, the reader is tossed between the thoughts of Baby Suggs and her daughter-in-law Sethe, with all the incomplete detail and unexplained allusion of close third person that obliges the reader to accept, for now, the partial truths being offered. At this stage, for example, the reader knows nothing of Sethe's history or relationships, of anywhere beyond the house or any context for the story, yet we are offered glimpses of all these things as they swirl around the character's head: 'Sethe smiled. This is the way they were – had been. All of the Sweet Home men, before and after Halle, treated her to a mild brotherly flirtation, so subtle you had to scratch for it'.[25]

In a work that moves back-and-forth between narratorial authority and different characters' inner lives in this way, slowly constructing what might be taken as truth from the fragmentary revelations of multiple perspectives, the writer's role is to shepherd the reader through the maze of thoughts and impressions, in much the same way as counsel undertakes to guide both witness and jury through the labyrinth of a complex case, highlighting what might be important, skirting over distractions or contradictions. In *Beloved*, many of the most difficult events experienced by the characters manifest initially as omissions and silences, the trauma of slavery resisted in the minds of Sethe, Paul D and Baby Suggs, and held back from the reader. But just as a lawyer might probe a witness to reveal what is concealed or protected in their original testimony, to unearth a possible 'truth', so the writer presses on with excavating what lies buried in the stories provided by her characters. In the case of *Beloved*, the reader is confronted with the details of Sethe's attack on her own children, which she has studiously obscured in her own narrative but which the narrator finally discloses through the indifferent eyes of 'the four horsemen' tracking her down: 'Then all four started toward the shed. Inside, two boys bled in the sawdust and dirt at the feet of a woman holding a blood-soaked child to her chest with one hand and an infant by the heels at the other'.[26] The crime Sethe has refused to admit, even to herself, other witnesses have attested to. The partial knowledge disclosed to the reader through her point of view is shown to be lacking, requiring the intervention of the narrator to establish a complete version of events and recalling the ways in which the court probes witness silences and suppressions to reach what it, too, considers a comprehensive account.

As the novel progresses, the characters' control over their stories unravels, and the narration becomes increasingly erratic. Thoroughly enmeshed in the characters' thoughts, it slips easily back and forth between omniscient third, close third and first-person points of view. In an extended passage when Sethe walks through town after a shift at work, for example, the reader is sucked from a bird's eye view of her 'wrapped tight, hunched forward, as she started home her mind was busy with the things she could forget' directly into her thoughts: 'You know I never would a left you. Never. It was all I could think of to do'. Bringing the character's internal voice directly to the reader in this way increases the emotional power of the writing and by the end of the novel, the intensity of emotion and pain experienced by Sethe and Beloved cause the further break down of any narratorial distance: several chapters are recited directly in the first person in the shattered and difficult language of a tormented mind. These short chapters might perhaps be compared to witness testimony in the courtroom, evoking sympathy in the reader/viewer and harnessing the energy of unmediated emotion but requiring an authoritative contextualization. In *Beloved*, these chapters, both beginning 'I am Beloved and she is mine', act as an emotional climax but nonetheless, the omniscient narrator is re-established for the final section of the story, provoking the reader from a distance to consider wider responsibilities of collective memory. The novel ends as it began, with an impersonal summary, this final commentary eliding Beloved's fate and the legacy of slavery: 'so they forgot her. Like an unpleasant dream during a troubling sleep'. In the courtroom, the lawyer similarly reworks the first-person witness account into a wider narrative, framing it through a third-person retelling so as to make a case about guilt or innocence. In the trial of the Sudanese military commander, Ali Muhammad Ali Abd-Al-Rahman, indicted for war crimes at the International Criminal Court, for example, the prosecuting counsel repeatedly wove witness statements into a more assured and informed narrative, recalling Morrison's fiction technique in the slippage between first-person and third:

> I would wish to emphasise children. For far too long, far too often, they have been the invisible casualties of war, conflated with the civilian population or just ignored. But the effect on them is profound, and it remains profound and lasting ... I quote what the witness says ... "I saw two corpses; one boy was breastfeeding from his mother while she was dead. They were shot with ammunition." And when the investigator asked for clarification about what he meant, the witness continued: "This little boy was ... his mom was dead, and he was breastfeeding from her. His age should be four or five months." That is simply one example of the human tragedy that Your Honours will

be listening to in the course of this trial and adjudicating whether it is true and whether Mr Abd-Al-Rahman is responsible for that and other crimes.[27] The voice of the individual is here set by the lawyer into a longer time frame and spatial reality – 'far too long'; 'far too often' – as he adopts the witness testimony into his sweeping narrative of 'the invisible casualties of war'. He raises the stakes: this is no longer a story about one casualty, seen through the eyes of one witness, but a more comprehensive narrative of the profound suffering of a civilian population viewed from the distance of The Hague and presented from the point of view of international justice.

Detaching the Intimate

Your character goes on a day trip. On the journey home, they are involved in an accident – a car crash, a train derailment, a fall… They're not seriously hurt, but they're understandably shaken and upset. When they get home, they recount the episode in their diary. Write this diary entry, adding as much detail as you can, and paying attention to the language they use to describe their experience and the feelings it prompted.

Now rewrite this diary entry as a document intended to give information to a legal team dealing with the accident. Use an omniscient third-person narration for this, but incorporate quotations directly from the diary entries – these quotations will retain the first-person narrative. Consider how the first-person extracts can be used to best effect. How can the narrator employ them to help build their argument? How can you differentiate the narrator's voice from the diary voice?

Ellipses and silences are fundamental to the way the storytelling operates in *Beloved*. The novel gradually fills the characters' lapses and omissions and in so doing breaks down the reader's sense of any single trustworthy perspective on events. How do we know who to believe if both characters and narrator are withholding information, or attributing different meanings to what remains undisclosed? The passages of close third-person narration reinforce this slipperiness as we become party to characters' intense questioning of the fundamental nature of the story they've been part of, including their own role in it. As Paul D reflects on his enslaved years towards the end of the novel, for example, he unearths insistent questions that he has formerly repressed but that now clamor for an answer and that in turn lay bare the novel's wider interrogation of slavery and its legacy: 'Oh, he did many things, but was that Garner's gift or his own will? What would he have been anyway – before Sweet Home – without Garner? In Sixo's country, or his mother's? Or, God help him, on the boat? Did a white man saying make it so?'[28] This tumble of questions recalls the rhetorical strategies of the legal statements quoted earlier in the chapter – the Old Bailey case reviewed in *Chambers Student*, for example, or the language employed in Skorinko's series of mock trials – in which questions are not employed with the aim of extracting an answer or gathering information but as a way of processing what's been heard and learnt and stimulating a new way of looking at the material:

> But wait, our barrister pointed out: look at him, strolling down the street, relaxed, seemingly happy – does this really look like someone who's about to commit a murder? And what about that 'no comment' interview revealing the defendant's uncooperative nature? Hold on, hold on. He did, unlike his co-defendant, turn himself in to the police – surely that shows cooperation if nothing else?[29]

Here, the barrister's aim can be read in much the same way as Morrison's intentions, interrogating and ultimately subverting the story that has been constructed to this point: 'It places a big, fat question mark over an opponent's argument, a persistent "what if?"', notes *Chambers Student*. 'Every utterance is geared towards provoking uncertainty.'[30]

As well as prompting doubt and re-evaluation, the use of questions also projects the reader into the most faltering and secreted elements of a character's psychology, particularly when close third-person narratives slip into passages of free indirect discourse, thoughts rising spontaneously as a response to a character's deepest internal struggles. As we've seen with Emma Bovary and Paul D, it is when characters are most frustrated and agonized that they throw questions back at themselves; the writer stacks multiple questions to highlight psychological conflict and distress. In court, a comparable salvo of questions can similarly be used to reveal intense emotional states. Challenging the prosecution's assertion in the Old Bailey trial that the defendant's continual reply of 'no comment' during interrogation is an indicator of coolness or disinterest, the defence barrister focuses instead on primal emotion: 'But what would you do if you were a 15-year-old? Scared, in a police station, accused of murder?'[31] The switch of point of view, expressed in the potency of the interrogative, is ultimately aimed at uncovering emotional authenticity by asking the jury to place themselves in the head of a terrified teenager.

Used in this way to disrupt narrative assumptions and reveal emotional state, questions employed in both fiction and court are usually intended to stand without response, being offered as an indicator of psychological dilemma rather than probing for answers, but of course the posing of questions that require an answer is also fundamental to courtroom practice, providing the framework on which a case is built and heard. Both the defence and the prosecution are given extended opportunities to question witnesses; in turn, witnesses are required to respond. By predicting and managing these responses, experienced counsel guides the witness testimony and in so doing, further moulds the story being constructed. A lawyer's own words cannot constitute evidence, but by choosing which questions to ask, and so which answers to elicit, counsel effectively layers their narrative point of view over the witness account, creating a complex double perspective that recalls the fictional 'dual voice' already highlighted. The immediate first-person testimony of the respondent/witness is enclosed within, and constrained by, the more knowing narrative fabricated by the interrogator/lawyer; despite being formed as a series of questions, the lawyer asks the jury to accept their overwriting of the witness story as authoritative. If a witness recognizes that the lawyer is actually the one telling the story and cedes control of point of view, this tends to result in a harmonious presentation of the facts, but if a witness makes the not unreasonable assumption that they are the narrator telling their own story in their own words, then inevitably a struggle ensues as perspectives fail to fully align. Examining the experiences of lay witnesses in court, Anita Barry describes this dynamic as 'a hidden level of conflict' that 'frustrates lawyers and witnesses alike and may affect the perceptions of jurors and ultimately the outcome of trials'.[32]

In his analysis of courtroom questioning strategies, the legal scholar Bader Nasser Aldosari highlights the ways in which a lawyer can use questions to apply her point of view over the evidence provided by a witness, noting how such a technique might encourage witnesses to fully reveal their stories while also dexterously allowing the interrogator to 'share their own stories and recount incidents from a legal standpoint'.[33] He suggests that well-constructed questions act as a vehicle for lawyers to position their version of events at the forefront of the jury's mind, drawing particular attention to 'so' questions and 'tag' questions, which he describes as having a 'coercive quality'. Both are posed as statements, restricting the witness to a simple 'yes' or 'no' answer: 'So, you try to leave the building at 5 but they prevented you?'; 'he didn't spend Christmas with you and your father in 1994. Is that right?'[34] As Aldosari discusses, this form of questioning draws the court into the narrative point of view proposed by the lawyer who tenders 'a statement containing the proposition they wish to advance, and then the question that follows compels the listener to confirm (by affirming or negating) the proposition the user advanced. As a result ... the declarative statement asks for the declarative to be confirmed'. While the purpose of these questions appears to be to elicit an answer, then, in fact they are posed with the intention of emphasizing and validating a particular point of view: 'the purpose of questioning tactics in court is to win rather than assist the court in gathering evidence'.[35]

Coercive Qualities

You're a parent of a ten-year-old boy and you're preparing for a custody hearing after a lengthy divorce battle. Draft a series of open questions that your legal team can ask you in court. These will allow you to explain why the judge should award you custody of your son. You might include questions about home (e.g. what are the living arrangements in your house?), school (e.g. how do you engage with parent-teacher meetings?) and personal details (e.g. what do you do with your son at weekends?). Be as thorough and detailed as possible. What are the best questions to show your case in a good light? How can you use questions to persuade the judge of your point of view?

Imagine that you are on the opposing legal team, representing your ex, and an admin mistake means that you've been sent the list of questions. Redraft them all as closed questions. These will also be asked in court, with the intention of changing the way the information is perceived (e.g. So, your son lives with you and a partner you've only known for two months, is that right? Is it correct that you find parent–teacher meetings stressful? You work shifts at weekends – is that right?)

Which set of questions gives the court most information and offers the most evidence? Which questions are the strongest and most likely to impact the outcome of the case?

In my conversations with courtroom experts and professionals, it's this focus on winning a case that is consistently emphasized, as you would expect. All my discussions circle back to the ways in which linguistic choices, including effective control of point of view, can determine the outcome of a case, which, unlike in fiction, can radically change people's freedoms and futures. At the end of his memoir, *A Dutiful Boy*, Mohsin Zaidi writes how his job as a criminal barrister is to 'tell a story … drawing together different threads to present a beginning, a middle and an end', but he emphasizes not the technical challenge of this process but the real-life jeopardy: 'A story can send someone to prison. It can be the tale of a life ruined and the telling of it can also ruin lives'.[36] In our discussions, Keith Belzer points out that it's precisely because those involved in a court case have so much to lose that the implications of changing points of view are so subtle and potent. He's clear that this is not about 'playing games' in court but about 'advancing the theory of innocence … seeing the case through the point of view of someone who is innocent, not presuming they're guilty'. In view of this claim, we discuss notions of truth and trust. Speaking to the *Paris Review*, the novelist Hernán Díaz described point of view as a 'clear example of trust in fiction' – the reader is engaging in an act of trust with the writer, he explains, which can be betrayed if the conventions are 'violated': 'I foam at the mouth whenever a narrator suddenly becomes omniscient just to present us with some cheap reveal'.[37] This notion of trust, I suggest to Keith, is particularly pertinent to a court of law, with its commitment to truth. In reply, he emphasizes how the rules of evidence and clear ethical guidelines commit lawyers to telling the truth in court, so that, while facts can be interpreted, nothing false can be claimed – this would be an act of perjury. So defence lawyers can be creative, he says, but 'the jury has to trust you'. When he proposes strategies for making a client's point of view explicit – as in the reconstructed cell experiment – it's important to understand the fundamental grounding in truth; this is not, he stresses, 'about making things up'. Creating a change of perspective, however, to present evidence to those in court from a different angle is not, he suggests, about obscuring or distorting truth, but rather about unearthing truths that may have been masked by usual court processes, or that a jury might not have considered, or wanted to consider. The point, he emphasizes, is not to show off 'a cheap reveal' but to create a shared understanding much like a reader builds up with a writer they trust. He maintains that managing point of view effectively highlights rather than conceals the more complete experience that underpins any case, allowing the facts to speak for themselves so that, in the end, the truth becomes evident and 'there's no way of seeing any alternative'.

Despite the clear power of these fictional techniques to assert, or manipulate, truth, the role of the writer's craft in legal practice barely ever gets a mention. While Keith includes short sessions on storytelling in his training for public defenders, law schools in general are slow to consider these areas in any detail. The idea that legal proceedings represent a form of narrative has gained some ground in the last twenty years – the law school at St Mary's University in London, for example, includes a 'law stories' module that examines the narrative techniques employed by courtroom dramas in film and on TV – but attention to what Keith terms 'the refined ideas' of fictional craft has generally been slight. The unwillingness of traditional law schools to examine these skills, however, means that in practice, many law professionals are juggling point of view in the courtroom without a clear sense of the powerful effect this might have or how the shifts might operate or accrue meaning.

In his practice, Keith frequently draws on the work of Joseph Campbell and Christopher Vogler, literary critics who explore narrative structure and storytelling extensively. He maintains that legal professionals could learn a great deal from close attention to fiction techniques (as well as film, with its deft manoeuvring of point of view through the camera). An understanding of how fiction works is important, he says, echoing my earlier conversation with Supardi Supardi, because 'whoever tells the best story will win', and the best story is inevitably one that has emotional impact. Writers, he says, are good at understanding that our experience is driven as much by character as event, and that it's when we see something through a character's eyes that it has greatest emotional impact. This emotional impact, made possible in the adept handling of point of view and perspective, is what will, in the end, carry the day in the all-important matter of winning a case: 'it isn't until we're immersed in the story that we cry', he says. 'You've got to get the court to that place'.

6

Worldbuilding/ Botanical Science

The Victorian painter, critic and writer, John Ruskin, had a polymath's passion for subjects as diverse as the structure of birds' wings, workers' education and political economy, but much of his thinking revolved around a fascination with scale: how the scrutiny of very small things might lead to a better understanding of much larger ones. His watercolours of oak leaves, mossy riverbanks and feathers record close observations of the natural world; by studying these, he suggested, we might not only better appreciate the beauty of nature but also grasp ideals of craftsmanship, the interconnectedness of human activity and the value of social ties. His recommendation that art students examine the fine detail of mineral specimens – the composition, form and texture – was predicated on the belief that this would lead to a realization of the complexity of much greater geological phenomena, and, by extension, the wider environment: 'A stone, when it is examined', he maintained, 'will be found a mountain in miniature'.[1]

This interplay of detailed observation and panoramic vision will be familiar to fiction writers. We've already considered how a similar dynamic might provide a basis for writing time, and we've seen its influence in the construction of character and plot. In this chapter I'll be exploring its particular relevance to the evocation of place through a process that is often called worldbuilding – that is, fully imagining a fiction setting that is so coherent, comprehensive and convincing that it springs to life as a fully formed world. This ability to conjure a vivid setting forms an important part of the writer's toolbox for all kinds of fiction. Creating and describing a place that feels authentic to the story and characters, and which the reader can see, hear, feel and fully experience, is a fundamental element of the storyteller's craft. But while realist fiction can draw on the writer's and reader's shared knowledge of the actual world, speculative fiction, especially science fiction and fantasy, frequently chooses to construct an alternative world from scratch. Even while elements might remain familiar, most of the features – including a history, culture and geography and, most relevantly for this chapter, a flora and ecology – are reshaped or completely reimagined in the act of writing.[2]

Constructing such a world for a work of fiction is a multilayered and expansive act that, as Ruskin proposed, requires a polymathic immersion in natural, social and political environments but also the ability to draw the reader's eye to the evidence and suggestion of telling detail. To help me explore this process, I'm focusing this chapter on the work of botanical scientists, and the interaction between the large and small on which their practice often depends. Just as in the first chapter I considered how archaeologists juggle illuminating moments with the elusive sweep of deep time, so in the construction of a plant's 'life story', botanists rely on both the reading of detail – often at a microscopic level – and a broader examination of the connections between specimens, species, habitats and environments in a global context.

This focus on botanical science also reflects the way in which plants dominate every terrestrial environment. Plants represent around 80 per cent of the biomass on earth. From gardens, city trees and parks to the great natural wildernesses at the edge of common experience, from the microscopic to the talismanic, we are surrounded by vegetation. Not surprisingly, then, writing a convincing plant world is often fundamental to the success of worldbuilding in a piece of fiction. But this omnipresence can also mean that we can take plant life for granted and, in effect, stop looking. Science has identified 'plant blindness', which may be ancestrally derived, and which naturally draws our attention to animals at the expense of plants. This intrinsic bias means that we might even struggle to recognize plants as being alive. Perhaps unsurprisingly, this everyday phenomenon has been traced through to fiction, with plant life being described as a 'narrative blindspot': 'the mysterious intricacies of vegetal lives … are largely cast aside'.[3]

Here, then, my reading of Ruskin proves helpful. Ruskin drew and painted a range of plants and flowers, collected specimens, recorded habitats and filled his library with books on botany. This fascination reflected the preoccupation with scale that we've already noted: Ruskin's concern was to discover both precise information about how plants grow, and the implicit moral and social implications of their habits. But it also acted as a way of seeing – making sure that we notice the world around us and using the act of seeing as a means of thinking about how this world works: 'to see clearly is poetry, prophecy, religion, all in one', he famously noted.[4] It's this holistic approach that I'm taking as my starting point in considering the technical challenges of worldbuilding, following in Ruskin's footsteps to turn a close eye on plants, discussing with botanical scientists how we interact with the vegetal and what role fiction might play in shaping the study of the crops, weeds, trees, flowers, roots, stems and seeds around us.

Plant life has a very long literary tradition, acting as both setting and metaphor across form and genre. In Dante's fourteenth-century poem, *The Inferno*, those who die by suicide are transformed into gnarled trees that bleed disturbingly when even the smallest of twigs is snapped. In Shakespeare's *Richard II* (1595), the queen and her lady in waiting overhear the palace gardeners bemoaning a 'disordered spring' of unruly fruit trees and overgrown herbs and ornamentals, an extended metaphor for Richard's failure to adequately manage his kingdom. Later, poets such as John Clare moved away from symbolism to draw on the physical and sensory reality of the natural world, but the Gothic imagination revelled in a return to metaphor, easily transposing visceral fears onto plant life, and breeding sinister plants that posed a threat to humans. With the boom in the exotic plant market and perilous plant-hunting expeditions in the nineteenth century, writers became fascinated with how the plant world might reflect and express darker imperatives and emotions. By the turn of the century, ravenous vines, predatory flycatchers and poisonous blossoms were springing from the soil to menace and attack: H. G. Wells' *The Flowering of the Strange Orchid* (1905), for example, tells of a plant collector who buys the last samples of a rare Southeast Asian plant, which turns out to emit a deadly soporific scent while it leeches blood from its victims with its tentacle-like roots. In the middle of the twentieth century, films such as *The Body Snatchers* (1955) and its sequel, *Invasion of the Body Snatchers* (1956; 1978), looked to radical traditions in botanical writing that challenged human primacy.[5] Moving towards and into this century, popular memoirs with a botanical theme have broadened the ways in which we think of plants to include encounters with troubling histories of colonialism, enslavement, genocide and extinction: in *My Garden (Book)*, for example, novelist Jamaica Kincaid explores a tension between the pleasure of tending for a garden and the colonial legacy of botany.

An interesting thread of current debate, however, is moving away from positioning plants as silent witness to, or metaphor for, human deeds, towards considering them instead on their own terms, without a need to anthropomorphize or connect them to our history and experience. Recognizing that plants exist in a unique time frame, completely asynchronous with ours, and highlighting the distinctly unhuman needs and interactions of vegetation, this approach immediately emphasizes botanical strangeness. Such an alien nature can be difficult for us to grasp and has been described by the influential French botanist, Francis Hallé, as 'an absolute alterity with regard to humans'.[6] But when plants are no longer reduced to objects of knowledge or food production, or a kind of inert green backdrop, this more radical perspective places them firmly within a worldview that requires an imaginative leap. Approaching plants in this way allows us to glimpse life forms that operate without human intervention – indeed, exist better without human interference – and which don't match up to the usual human measures. Fiction is, inevitably, human-centric: as readers we're interested in characters and relationships, we enjoy making connections to our own ways of living, we understand story as it connects to the events that shape us. But by exploring what it is to be human, fiction also allows for, perhaps even demands, reflection on what might exist at the very edge of our experience, or beyond it. If we accept that plants have natures that are radically different to our own and which we don't even fully understand, then the way we write plant life becomes a way of investigating and proposing alternative attitudes to, and experiences of, community, culture, politics, morality and being.

This view of plants as unfamiliar other rather than everyday encounter not only draws the curious eye back to notice the plant life around us but also offers a new way of conceiving of, and representing, place in our writing, fusing most obviously with the work of speculative fiction writers and their commitment to worldbuilding the strange and challenging. I'll be talking later in the chapter to speculative fiction specialists, but my first conversation begins by returning to questions of scale, and the attention to detail that often drives the botanist's understanding of their subject. I've connected with Nirupa Rao, who joins me from her elegant apartment in Bangalore. Nirupa is a botanical illustrator who specializes in portraying the unique ecosystems of the Western Ghats in her home state of Karnataka; I begin by asking how she considers the relationship between her exquisitely detailed observational works of individual specimens and a more expansive view of a mountain range that stretches for over 1600 km. She explains that she sees no tension between the two, but, like Ruskin, discerns an overarching coherence in which each is repeated in the other. She talks about all the creatures and organisms supported by a single tree, directing my attention to ever smaller life forms, all of which are interdependent. 'Every organism is a microcosm in itself', she says, 'the level of detail is infinite. Whether a tiny cell or an entire habitat, the principles are echoed'.

As we explore this idea of echo further, Nirupa turns, without my prompting, to fiction. This reiteration of the micro in the macro, the significance of a tiny observation for a larger conceptualization of the environment is, she explains, similar to the way in which place is successfully rendered in fiction; her view of the botany she studies is 'quite novelistic, the same story repeated on different scales'. She reads avidly and as we talk, she rummages through the bookshelves behind her and above her head to root out examples to help her make her points. She admires the novel form, she says, precisely because of its ability to employ intimate detail as an entry point to wider cultural or social issues – in this she identifies a clear parallel to her own work. While her artistic focus might be on a single flower or a few stems, she explains, 'my larger point and purpose is ecological health'. She finds particular connections in magical realism, which helps her grasp a sense of strangeness and the fantastical. By 'sliding just the other side of normality' through her reading, she says, she's been able to develop a way of thinking that allows her to access the lives of plants, becoming alert to detail that is mostly concealed or disregarded and conscious of possibilities taking place out of normal sight.

As we talk, I'm reminded of Arundhati Roy's 1997 novel, *The God of Small Things*, which is doused in the botanical richness of Kerala, at the southern end of the Western Ghats. Much as Nirupa aims to help us reimagine plant life through her meticulous illustrations of the region, so Roy draws the reader's eye from detail to detail as a way of reflecting the 'small things' of the title – the apparently insignificant events and decisions that shape the characters' lives in profound ways – and how these, in turn, are impacted by much larger movements outside the characters' immediate experience. Like Nirupa's artwork, Roy's novel is concerned with the relationship of the tiny to the huge. The novel opens with the clammy detail of a hot May day, a close focus on 'dissolute bluebottles' and 'dustgreen trees' as the river 'shrinks' in the heat at the end of the summer. But twenty-three years later, Rahel is confronted by the same river on her return from self-imposed exile and finds it wrapped in a green sheet that inhibits biodiversity. It's the rainy season, and the monsoons should be bringing the river and its plants to life, but it is

> no more than a swollen drain now. A thin ribbon of thick water that tapped wearily at the mud banks on either side, sequined with occasional silver of a dead fish. It was choked with a succulent weed, whose furred brown roots saved like thin tentacles under water ... a slow, slugging green ribbon lawn that ferried garbage to the sea.[7]

By forcing us to look at the detail of 'bronze winged lily-trotters' in this 'slow green ribbon', Roy inevitably draws our attention to larger forces of neglect, pollution and untrammelled industrialization.

In my conversation with Nirupa, she acknowledges the impact of these large external factors, explaining how she views her generation in particular (she's in her mid-twenties) as dangerously divorced from nature. 'It's not something we consider our domain', she says. 'Plant knowledge is in serious decline'. The attention to detail in her work springs from the simple desire to help us observe in order both to address the dwindling of knowledge and raise more fundamental questions about our relationship with the natural world (and ourselves). Having trained in sociology, she tends to a broad, even evangelizing, view of creative practice that recalls Ruskin's concerns from more than a century earlier: 'as an artist, I want to change social behavior', she says.

'Scientific literacy is really important; I want to take science out of the ivory tower'. In this capacity to make botanical science accessible and engaging, she recognizes further 'echoes' with fiction. Her artwork can operate like fiction, she claims, to tackle our inability to recognize, and take an interest in, plants, underscoring their role in a meaningful environment and 'reinstating plant life in the popular imagination'.

As we talk, Nirupa returns to the value of the imaginative act, not so much to close the distance between ourselves and the botanical environment but rather to appreciate how large and unfathomable that distance might be. Too often, she points out, we look for resemblance to ourselves to help understand the plant world, but a more interesting approach is to accept and celebrate their difference. Plants, she says, need to be recognized as 'so different; the way they operate is obviously so advanced and on a completely different plane'. Through the studies she draws for her illustrations, she has come to recognize that plants behave as communities with what she terms 'lifestyles'. The fact that these lifestyles don't resemble ours is, for her, the challenge of rethinking place along completely new lines. The world we assume we're part of, and the worlds we build in our fiction, she explains, need to take account of the fact that these lifestyles might remain unknown and out of reach. 'We don't have to be able to relate to something to value it on its own terms', she says. Our apprehension of plants, she believes, comes down to one question: 'How much are we able to stretch our imaginations?'

Picture Postcard

Take a photo of a part of a plant – a leaf or flower, a stem or stamen. What do you notice when you look at the photo?

Now make a drawing of the same thing, preferably from life rather than the photo. Spend time aiming for as much accuracy and detail as possible. Have you noticed anything different about the specimen while drawing? How does it contribute to its habitat? What adaptation has this plant made to its environment? How is it part of an ecosystem?

Now imagine that you have found this specimen during an expedition. It has never been recorded before. Your photo and drawing are the only

> evidence to prove this plant exists. Write a postcard back to your research base sharing the news. You want to explain that the plant has a unique 'lifestyle' in relation to its environment, so that while it looks quite ordinary, it is in fact very strange. You have space for no more than 50 words on your postcard, plus this drawing and photo to enclose. What will you write? How will you explain your observations on habitat, environment and ecosystem to emphasize the unique strangeness of your discovery? What will you draw attention to in the pictorial evidence?

In his influential book, *The Environmental Imagination* (1996), Lawrence Buell, a pioneer of contemporary ecocriticism, foreshadowed my conversation with Nirupa by similarly positioning creative imagination as the most important element in facilitating new ways of understanding the natural world. The current environmental emergency, Buell suggested, was indicative of 'a crisis of the imagination' in which we fail to properly conceive of the plant world, falling back on easy assumptions of otherness or wilderness that allow us to dominate, exploit and marginalize; solutions to the emergency, he proposes, depend on finding better – and different – ways of imagining nature and our relation to it.[8] Buell argues that the creative arts are uniquely important in enabling this imaginative act since they not only reflect how a culture sees its relationship to the natural world but can, more significantly, determine it. In their 2019 work, *Radical Botany*, Natania Meeker and Antónia Szabari make a similar case for the creative dialogue plants allow with the material world, and the importance of plants to human experience. They echo Buell in highlighting how 'plants can destabilize, exceed, or bypass our limited human faculties', forcing us to engage in imaginative speculation to elicit their most powerful meanings.[9] This repeated critical observation of the inevitable and essential dynamic interaction between plants and imagination, the locating of botany in a space that requires a creative act to be understood, can help inform our practice as writers. But how do we approach these strange things in our fiction? What value is there for the reader in entering a world pervaded by plants? And how can we create stories that receive and understand place in a new way, animated by an interaction with vegetable life?

In an attempt to unpick some of these questions, I've arranged an early morning call to New Zealand with Octavia Cade, whose research specialism is marine plants, particularly the reproductive strategies of *Zostera muelleri* seagrass; she also publishes speculative fiction exploring science and environment. We begin by discussing how the two practices intersect, at which point Octavia launches into a critique of scientific papers, which, she suggests, 'are the worst tool on the planet. They're designed so the minimum number of people can understand them'. Her interest in science communication, and particularly in writing fiction, stems from a reaction to these inaccessible and unhelpful publications. Her practice as a writer, as she sees it, is to investigate and interpret the brilliance of science 'without the jargon and exclusivity', reinstating imagination into our assessment of the natural world in a way that, as Buell suggests, might shape our responses to it. She hoards science research papers and news stories, she says, especially when they feature 'a weird plant or a weird ecosystem', and uses these as the inspiration for her creative work. By reconfiguring the research into a new imaginative world, she can offer the reader a means of encountering the science not only in an accessible way but also as an integrated and fundamental element of the fiction process.

As a botany specialist, plants inevitably form an important part of Octavia's reimagining of science in her speculative fiction, but she recognizes that she's not unique in this focus. Writing about what she terms 'speculative vegetation', Katherine Bishop claims that plants are uniquely placed to inform speculative fictions because, when stripped of human contexts, they naturally become strange and alien, so allowing us to see beyond ourselves. Plants, Bishop argues, present a life form that 'transforms our attitudes', enabling readers to look beyond a simple binary of botanical and human to 'explore commonalities, hybridities and mutual forms of growth'.[10] When I ask Octavia about these transformative qualities in plants, she agrees. She employs the same term as Bishop – 'commonality' – as she highlights our habits of talking to plants and even playing them music, identifying particular specimens and giving them a sense of character. She reminds me that every one of us is 'part plant' in our microbiome and stresses that 'dealing with non-human life, like plants, is not just about other cultures and worlds but about our commonality'. On the other hand, as she explains, plants also offer a way of exploring these other cultures and worlds because they present 'a form of life so different from us'. It's this disjunction between the familiar or congruent and the utterly mysterious that, for Octavia, means plants generate a fertile creative space where the everyday collides with the strange.

As we discuss the ways in which this juxtaposition between the common and the outlandish can draw the reader into an absorbing fictional environment, Octavia emphasizes the importance of a vibrant and expansive vegetal connectivity. Echoing Nirupa's approach, she argues that fiction needs to fully integrate entire ecosystems rather than 'cherry picking' bits and pieces of plant life for the sake of adding colour or curiosity. It's the larger implications of plant life that allow the writer to challenge – and possibly transform – attitudes, she says, and 'when fiction is done badly, it's generally because the interactions between the ecosystems are very basic; the plant has only one function. This is so simplistic and not true'. It's impossible, she points out, to build a convincing world in this way: 'it would collapse. Organisms need to interact with each other'. She emphasizes the need to connect plants in fiction to everything around them – climate, water, microorganisms in the soil – and so begin to construct a world which might encourage the reader to rethink our own.

This commitment to connecting the individual specimen to larger questions of environment and ecosystem resonates with the concept of 'radical botany' proposed by Meeker and Szabari. In their exploration of speculative fiction, they present an understanding of plant life as a catalyst for change; plants, they claim, act as 'the vehicle of speculation about human social and political life ... an engine of social critique and speculations about possible futures'.[11] They place 'new fictions' at the heart of this process of shifting ingrained attitudes, drawing attention again to the potential of imaginative connection. These 'new fictions', they argue, allow us to 'imagine, think and visualize ways of disassembling our socially and historically located subjectivities', enabling us to address pressing crises, such as global heating and environmental degradation.[12] When Octavia and I explore this idea of 'new fictions', she is quick to highlight the potential of storytelling to help us view our planet and its systems in new ways, but she points to a pitfall in what she calls 'the encyclopaedic aspect' of such a project.

The tendency for novels to become huge and unwieldy in their desire to fully represent the science and its implications for entire worlds is a problem, she says, for both writer (whose project spirals beyond reasonable control) and reader (who might struggle to hold all the novel's elements in their minds). As a solution, she offers an old-fashioned sense of wonder. While the writer needs to present the basic science, she maintains, they also need to 'smash the sense of wonder hard' so that the reader must 'want this ecosystem to exist so badly that they don't care about the details'. I consider whether the scientist, with her commitment to detail and evidence, is at odds here with the writer's willingness to dodge unworkable elements in a desire to evoke a passionate response in the reader, but Octavia is clear that 'fudging' some of the science is acceptable if this compels the reader to confront the key questions of our times.

Offering a justification for this compromise, Octavia points out that our knowledge of the natural world is not definitive or complete, with new discoveries constantly being made and new questions coming to the fore. She highlights recent examples of research identifying the alphabet structure underlying whale song, or establishing the existence of entangled underground networks of fungi. It's by rummaging in these uncertainties and partialities that the writer finds space to work, she maintains. She doubles down on the idea of wonder, explaining how her research with seagrass is concerned with a 'vast colonial organism in a great sprawling form', which is a continual source of wonder for her as a writer. It's this wonder that allows her to speculate and question. In this context, she raises the debate about plant sentience, explaining how she would 'love to think that there's a sentient community here' in the colonies of seagrass but that, as a scientist, she 'has no evidence; I have to keep rational'. It's by harnessing the writer's wonder to propose possibilities beyond the evidence, however, that her work comes together, each discipline nudging the other. She points out that the creative process that enables her fiction – and the worlds it allows her to imagine – offers a valuable touchstone for the questions tentatively dared by science. 'There's a long history of stories where plants are sentient', she points out, 'and now this is beginning to pay off in real science. It's hard to be sure – it may be wishful thinking – but the idea has been in writers' minds for ages'.

Writing at the edges of known plant science, then, can propel an emotional reaction in the reader while also prompting intellectual debate by acting as the 'vehicle of speculation about human social and political life' proposed by Meeker and Szabari. In order to consider this dual potential in more detail, I'm turning to Pat Murphy's 1985 short story, 'The Vegetable Wife', which tackles the 'wonder' of plant sentience raised by Octavia. It introduces us to Fynn, 'a square-jawed man with coarse brown hair and stubby, unimaginative fingers', who we first see planting the seed he's purchased for a vegetable wife. The package has arrived with generic instructions: 'Prefers sandy soil, sunny conditions. Plant two inches deep after all danger of frost has passed'.[13] Other horticultural options, we're told, are available, including Vegetable Bride and Vegetable Maiden, offering only slightly more sexualized versions of the anthropomorphized marketing names we're familiar with from our own seed packets: 'White Lady' runner beans, for example, or 'Dancing Geisha' dianthus. Fynn's unidentified world is simply drawn, similar to our own but with some subtle difference, including a 'living dome' providing housing and a 'green sky', but recognizable in its abundance of plant life: Fynn survives by tending a crop of a plant called cimmeg to provide both food and medicine. Beyond the cimmeg farm is a 'vast expanse' of native grassland that shifts and hisses in the wind, irritating Fynn so much with its noise 'like people whispering secrets' that he delights in hacking it down, echoing our own history of colonial destruction.

The plant life in Fynn's world, then, is, on the one hand, conventional but on the other unsettling, lending a sense of disquiet – both literally and figuratively – which grows in the reader as the vegetable wife grows in her pot. Fynn's brutal desecration of the grassland becomes amplified in his attitude towards his plant wife as she grows into a recognizably female form: in a series of incidents of increasing sexual violence, he gropes and assaults her; restrains her with a tether, which causes her to bleed 'pale sap'; beats, whips and rapes her. His violence is casual and dehumanizing (she is, after all, a plant), justified in his mind by her passivity and lack of expression: she does not 'fight back'; she cannot speak; her face is invariably 'impassive' and her expression 'that of a sleep-walker, an innocent young girl who wanders in the dark unawares'. The instructions with the seed packet have reassured him that she feels no pain. Without these human cues, Fynn cannot understand her, nor respond to her with any sensitivity; she is beyond him, too different and unknowable. The compassion he feels in the early days as he watches her mature quickly dissipates when she fails to behave in a way he recognizes; an element of his violence is directed at trying to evoke some kind of human reaction in her. When a young government inspector notes that such wives are 'quite sensitive, I hear', Fynn can only shrug.

Murphy's story is disturbing and uncomfortable, not only because its subject matter is, on one level at least, domestic violence, but also because it forces the reader to rethink her attitudes towards plants. Like Fynn's wife, the plants around us do not speak or show expression; they do not respond to us in human terms. As the story makes clear, however, such inscrutability does not mean we can impose our will and needs upon them, or dismiss any possible alternative methods they might have for expressing inner states, sensations or desires. The vegetable wife in Murphy's fiction is portrayed as part of the wider botanical community of the planet, 'the wind in her hair, like the wind in the tall grasses', which Fynn also cuts down, in this way acting not only as a metaphor for the female body in a patriarchal society or as a site of colonial violence but also forcing us to reconsider the traditional hierarchy, which disregards and subordinates the entire vegetal ecosystem as insensate and disposable. By turning our attention to the detail of one plant and her distress, Murphy conjures the reality of both this speculative world and our own, summoning a wider sense of place in the existence of such a seed packet and raising difficult questions about agency and moral autonomy. Fynn's violence is ultimately predicated on a failure of imagination. This 'methodical man' cannot stretch his thinking, as Nirupa advocates, to accommodate a life form that does not correspond to his limited preconceptions.

Our reading of 'The Vegetable Wife' supports Bishop's claim that plant life in science fiction can be transformative. It forces us to revisit our attitudes to sexuality, offering a feminist discourse on what it might mean to be consumable, in the way we presume vegetation is. In Fynn's world, as in ours currently, it's necessary to eat plants to survive, but the story poses the question of what this fact might mean for broader issues of consumption. It also, and perhaps most obviously, raises questions about the possibility of sentience in plants, and even intelligence. At the end of the story, when the vegetable wife finally reacts to Fynn's cruelty and exacts revenge for his violence towards her, her actions are presented as conscious and deliberate: she applies 'slow steady pressure' to his throat and 'clung to him until his struggles stopped'. Her relief feels relatable as she stands in the sun by the window and gazes out, speculating on what might grow when she, in turn, plants Fynn as she has watched him plant seeds.[14] The capacity to feel pain is apparently extended to the ability to experience other emotions – longing, loneliness, desire – and to encompass a capability for reasoning. In solving the problem of what to do about Fynn and her unbearable situation, the vegetable wife appears to demonstrate intelligence.

In my conversations with Nirupa and Octavia, both have raised these questions of intelligence as a natural extension of their thinking. For Nirupa, the issue of plant intelligence is so obvious as to be 'almost irrelevant'; it's simply a matter of reframing what we consider intelligence to be – 'why' she asks, 'should they have the same kind of intelligence as us?' Octavia expresses a warier approach informed by her scientific research but admits a wish for plant intelligence to be proven: 'all the work indicating that there's some form of intelligence might come to nothing but we're in a liminal place informed by love and hope'. Since liminal places offer such potential for fiction, and since the notion of some kind of sentient plant life has been influential in numerous stories, it's worth exploring these ideas further. Do we, as writers, need to consider plants as characters with agency? How can we best explore and write contemporary research about plant intelligence?

Can Plants Think?

If a plant was able to think, how would we recognize this ability? What might these thoughts look like? What purpose would they serve? Could a plant be able to think but unable to experience emotion? How might a plant experience physical sensation, such as heat or pain? Is a plant's ability to think hampered by its lack of motor function (i.e. its ability to execute voluntary movements)?

How might we compare possible plant intelligence to artificial intelligence?

> If we accepted that plants are intelligent and/or sentient, how would that change our relation to them? Does science fiction help us imagine such a possibility?
>
> Debate these questions with a partner or in a small group. Then agree on an approach and draft a post to an online research site, explaining your shared viewpoint and the reasons behind it. What happens if you can't agree? Can you identify the key points of dispute? How might you articulate these in the online post?

The notion that plants might demonstrate a form of intelligence, and can be discussed using terms such as consciousness, memory and intention, draws significant criticism from many scientists who suggest this language is misdirected in its anthropomorphism; others draw attention to what they see as 'a foolish distraction' dependent on 'over-interpretation' and 'wild speculations' that tend towards irrationality and animism.[15] On the other side of the debate, however, some commentators suggest that what is required is a reimagining of the nature of plants and a repositioning of language, suggesting like Nirupa that we need to ask how far (and why) plant sentience should resemble our own. Michael Pollan points out, for example, that our tendency to equate behaviour with physical movement, facial expression and speaking prevents us from seeing plants as 'behaving', as does the fact that we struggle to grasp the time frame in which they exist.[16] In their 2015 book, *Brilliant Green: The Surprising History and Science of Plant Intelligence*, botanist and 'plant neurobiologist' Stefano Mancuso and journalist Alessandra Viola argue that it is cultural prejudice rather than scientific evidence that prevents us acknowledging plants as intelligent beings. They suggest that it's because botanical processes and movements are often imperceptible that we assume plants are inert, impassive and unfeeling, like Murphy's vegetable wife. But urging us to look more closely, they propose a notion of plant intelligence as networked, with multiple command centers, operating in a not dissimilar manner to the internet; they identify plants as intelligent based on an ability to solve problems and act as a community. They point out that plants are 'able to receive signals from their environment, process the information, and devise solutions adaptive to their own survival' while demonstrating sensory ability to orientate themselves by interacting with other plants, as well as insects and humans, communicating with each other and even exhibiting 'various character traits'.[17] Comparing plant activity to the 'swarm intelligence' shown by insects and human crowds, *Brilliant Green* makes a case for re-evaluating botanical science to take account of the complex interior lives of plants.

This argument remains highly speculative and controversial, but nonetheless, in the ten years since Mancuso and Viola's book was published, the idea has gained some ground. Recent work on fungi, as Octavia discussed with me, has emphasized the mycelium network that connects with tree roots to transfer water, nitrogen and minerals and that demonstrates a form of communication through electrical signalling. The Basque philosopher and environmentalist, Michael Marder, has published a number of papers emphasizing a view of plant life as dynamic and sentient, each plant existing, he claims, as 'not only an inert what, but also a who … a whisperer of its peculiar knowledge, a center of intelligence or an agent capable of behaving in one way or another'.[18] While much of the scientific community may oppose the notion of plants as such centres of intelligence, the dialogue about what constitutes sentience and how we understand life forms so different from our own continues to stimulate nuanced debate to challenge the rigid and long-standing hierarchies between botanical and mammal life forms. For fiction writers, this debate not only offers fascinating insights on what it means to be alive but also creates opportunities to integrate plants into fiction in a powerful and active way.

With these possibilities in mind, I begin my final conversation, with Dr Jen Sloan, a biosciences researcher at the University of Sheffield. She joins me from her study at home, with her young daughter ferrying in a sandwich while we talk. We dive straight into discussion about plant intelligence and whether it's possible to detect any form of sentience in plants, and Jen is clear on her views: 'Are plants sentient? No. There's no evidence for that'. But she admits that the notion is both complicated and appealing. 'It's absolutely fascinating', she says. 'There are so many parallels with us communicating, us thinking. Plants can't think – but they can react so quickly to things'. She, too, offers the example of underground fungal networks, emphasizing the complexity of such natural connections and reflecting on how easy it can be for such networks to escape attention. 'Even as scientists', she says, 'we think about above ground. We don't think about underground. Everyone forgets'. It's these oversights and blind spots, she suggests, that allow for unexpected questions to emerge; in turn, these questions can prompt new ways of approaching evidence. 'The signalling cascade is constantly happening; a little plant living on the forest floor can switch on all of that machinery so quickly', she explains, pointing out that this is proven science. The remaining gaps in the knowledge of this process, however, provide space for speculation. In this case, Jen echoes Nirupa in proposing that what surfaces is a fundamental question about how we understand and define our perception of the natural world. She emphasizes that humans and plants are 'as unrelated from each other as things can be'. 'So', she concludes, 'it all boils down to – what is sentience?'

As a scientist, Jen says her work is driven by the need to find out exactly how plants work, which requires attention to the tiniest of details and functions. Her research on leaf growth takes place at a minute level, 'down to the individual cell', to explore ways of increasing leaf size and so improving yield; she's now looking at how microscopic openings in rice, known as the stomata, might be reduced in number so that the plants require less water and so become more resilient to drought conditions. For her, discovering the secrets of how these 'tiny bits' operate is inspirational. But she admits that immersing herself in the fine detail of botanical specimens it can become 'difficult not to get very narrowed down'. She returns to ideas of contrast in scale with which we began this chapter to explain how the discussion around plant sentience acts as an important foil to the intense focus on the microscopic that her research demands. Taking a step back to consider how her discoveries apply to crops, and then a further step back to consider the whole environment, is, she says, challenging but important, and the debate around plant intelligence offers a further opportunity to bring a wider lens to her research. When she applies this broader context to her thinking, she admits, notions such as plant sentience no longer 'feel like a massive leap'. The work she undertakes at cell level, she explains, reveals the enormous complexity of every specimen; spooling out to consider this complexity more expansively opens up, rather than closes down, possibilities. 'Plants are so complicated', she sighs, 'and so are we. This in itself should bring to mind all kind of questions and suggestions'.

In his recent work on plants, Michael Marder similarly highlights the complexity of plants, drawing direct comparison between their intricate constructions, the 'vast domains' in which they operate and the structures of storytelling. Plants create stories, he maintains, in their cycles of bloom and dormancy, their reactions to weather and disease, 'rendering witness accounts about life and death, light and darkness, middles, beginnings and ends'.[19] He links patterns of botanical growth to the structure of *mythos*, positioning the plant as both protagonist and narrator in its own sweeping story 'generational, flourishing, decaying, and regenerating – a cyclical movement that opens unto the vast domains of planetary time and soil composition, among other things'.[20] Other critics have considered how botanical issues such as invasive species, extinction or ecological decline create what has been termed 'vegetal agency', in which, again, plants are given the role of both central character and primary storyteller.[21] At the heart of this proposition is what we, as fiction writers, might recognize as worldbuilding. Marder draws our attention to how plants inevitably transport us to what he calls 'the milieu'.[22] Echoing Ruskin's thinking and Nirupa's recognition of repetitions of scale, he highlights the all-embracing nature of this 'milieu':

> [its] collaborations and collisions of plants with bacteria, fungi, and animals; agriculture and permaculture; diets and habitats; and, less and less so, the wilderness ... the blurry boundaries between communities and individuals in the vegetal world, where individual plants turn out to be thriving communities and plant communities come close to a single plant, for instance, by way of sharing the same root below ground.[23]

In this vibrant and profound layering of the above and below ground, the tiny and the large, the individual and the community, Marder compares the worlds constructed by botanical life directly to the worlds we build in fiction. His milieu is drawn from real-life botanical communities but can be extended to embrace, articulate and define our 'modes of inhabiting' fiction so that in his analysis, both are 'about ways of accessing the world in its being-world'.[24]

With these correspondences in mind, I turn my conversation with Jen to the specific challenges of worldbuilding. From her perspective as a researcher, I ask, does she believe that plants can be successfully rendered in fiction? Is it possible for the writer to capture the complexity and multiple scales of a vegetal world? We talk about regions such as the Amazon rainforest, where the rich variety of plant life requires no fictionalization to be rendered impressive, strange and even menacing. Here, worldbuilding has been fully taken care of by nature, and offers fiction a vibrant ready-made character, as Joseph Conrad's *Heart of Darkness* (1899) and similar jungle novels demonstrate. But just as effective, Jen suggests, are works that extract specimens or species from these kinds of abundant habitats to place them into what might be considered human environments, not only to look more closely at the individual behaviours of plants but also to draw attention to what happens if they transgress the roles traditionally assigned to them. She cites John Wyndham's *The Day of the Triffids* (1951, later a radio series, a film, and finally a TV series) as an example she's fond of. In Wyndham's post-apocalyptic vision, where most humans have been blinded by a rogue meteor shower, carnivorous ambulant plants take over the world, killing all those in their path. Even if the story now seems dated, Jen maintains that its commitment to creating a fully imagined situation predicated on, and determined by, the behaviours of plants shows what can be done when writers fully engage with what plants are and how they operate.

I press Jen further. Wyndham's *The Day of the Triffids* begins, I point out, with a discussion about how the farmed triffids demonstrate 'a well-developed intelligence' in the ways they choose to attack, with the narrator deciding 'it's likely to be an altogether different type of intelligence' than that displayed by humans.[25] This conversation seems to anticipate current debate, so, I ask, is it reasonable to claim that fiction can inform botanical science? Can Marder's explicit association of plant and story, for example, illuminate the work she does on biological microscopic activity? If writers adopt and reimagine these plant communities in order to conjure worlds that are both like our own and yet set apart, destabilized and asynchronous, will this change the science? Jen reflects on these points at some length before answering; her response is given with an encouraging smile. When the plant life in a fictional world is fully and convincingly imagined, she says, it can bring a new perspective to scientific research or reframe existing inquiries, becoming potent enough to challenge the accepted norms of botanical science. This means fictional works are important, she adds, because they can jolt us out of tired assumptions and force us to consider 'a different way of being'. Further to *The Day of the Triffids* example, she cites Roald Dahl's 1949 short story, 'The Sound Machine', a story that is similar in tone and approach to 'The Vegetable Wife'. In Dahl's tale, the invention of a machine to eavesdrop on plants allows us to hear the groans and screams as they are pruned and felled, with the implication that they feel pain. As Jen points out, this post-war short story was written long before scientists began to debate any notions of plant sentience, but the freedom and speculation possible in fiction enabled it to explore ideas that scientists had not yet tackled (or did not dare to). 'In a fictional world like the one Dahl gives us, you don't have to take a very big leap to make these connections', she says, 'and once it's out there, then it becomes possible to imagine other scenarios'.

For Jen, the power of fiction is its ability to propose such possibilities, highlighting in doing so 'the fact that we don't know the answers'. She identifies this 'not knowing' as a driver for both her work as a scientist and her reading of stories: the desire to know more, and to nurture an ambitious curiosity, underpins both. In particular, she returns to the importance of questions, especially fiction's ability to generate new and unexpected ones. When it comes to a better understanding of plants and the worlds they create, she says, 'we always need questions'. It's an alertness to these questions that, she suggests, connects the writer and the scientist; writing fiction and researching science should, she says, be viewed as complementary processes of discovery because 'imagination and questions and science should all be intertwined'. She finishes our conversation by emphasizing the importance of these creative connections. If we are to fully explore and understand the worlds built by and with plants, whether on the page, in the lab or in the wild, we need to communicate across disciplines and divides, she says. 'The only commonality we have with plants is being alive, so to understand what they are, we need to be open in asking, wondering, imagining – how can we grasp these weird life-forms and the outrageous worlds they create?'

Three Words

In emphasizing creative connections, Jen Sloane provides a helpful ending to a project that has been actively in search of the 'intertwinings' she advocates. The questions posed to my conversation partners have been occasioned by a desire to discover where fruitful correspondences are located and where I might be mistaken in thinking there are any. Mostly, not unexpectedly, there have been few definitive answers. The process of interrogation has been productive and inspiring, but generally we've found ourselves discussing probabilities and maybes, what-ifs and potentials. This is perhaps how it should be. This is how the best conversations progress.

Three words have figured consistently, however, during these conversations, providing a thread through this jumble of ideas. Unprompted by me, these three words have been employed by specialists from different disciplines and from different cultures, returned to again and again. These words are reader, humanness and imagination. Let's take them in turn.

Reader. The experts I've spoken to in the writing of this book have all turned instinctively to the role of the reader when trying to articulate the connections they see between their work and the processes at work in fiction. They've talked about what they read and how they read, and they've recognized the act of reading as a particularly flexible and nuanced mode of understanding. When we've talked about what the writer is doing in constructing a story, we've also talked about what the reader is doing in laying claim to it. While fiction writers are constantly and necessarily in dialogue with their reader, it may seem surprising that professionals in other fields are also finely attuned to the role of the reader, but in reaching for common ground between different disciplines it's perhaps inevitable that reading will play a part. On one level, this is because a lot of people read, while far fewer write. For my conversation partners, their experience and understanding of fiction was often informed by their role as reader, a useful reminder that writing of a piece of fiction only confers a kind of half-life, the story not fully coming alive until it is read and the reader has brought their own meanings to the words on the page. On a more significant level, however, this emphasis on reading highlights how the process of interaction and interpretation, the respectful yet slightly edgy relationship between writer and reader, offers a positive model for taking forward these interdisciplinary conversations. Reading, as the American writer Madeleine L'Engle has noted, provides a route 'into the expanding universe'; by becoming readers of each other's work, we are able to extend our ways of thinking and stretch our own practice.[1] Reading is a naturally symbiotic, interdisciplinary activity. At its most effective and pleasurable, it prompts us, as Barthes reminds us, 'to look up often, to listen to something else'; it takes us beyond ourselves 'like a cork on the waves'.[2] In this context, it was perhaps inevitable that my discussions returned time and again to reading. In picking our way between different disciplines, we do well to all harness the inquiry, wonder and energy of the talented reader.

Humanness. This project has been intended to establish writing as a fit co-participant in a range of respected and consequential 'real-life' activities, to challenge the way in which creative writing – and fiction in particular – is frequently perceived, which is too often as an activity adjacent to a 'real' world, an addition or an indulgence, a fancy. I've aimed to explore what happens if we install fiction and its processes in the engine room instead of confining it to a stool at the bar. I set out to investigate how and why fiction techniques are an important element in a range of activities, how they underpin diverse ways of thinking, and how we can make this proximity more explicit. I've tried to find out what happens when we insist that fiction matters, and not only when we're in search of a good read for the holidays.

In his analysis of urban fictions, the architect Colin Fournier reminds us that 'Reality needs fiction in order to probe the unknown and be prepared for the future … ' Fiction, he says, provides 'the evolutionary process behind mutations as well as one of the filters leading to the survival of the fittest ideas.'[3] Such comments reinstate fiction as critical to the interrogation and transformation of the ways in which we live, work and think; as a means of testing and sifting ideas, and as a force for change. They remind us that fiction is concerned with what it is to be human. It poses the crucial questions and helps us find a way, if not of answering them definitively, then of understanding why they need to be asked. In the discussions that have informed this book, we have kept coming back to this underlying curiosity about the nature of humanness across time, place and idea. What we've discovered is that this mutual fascination with humanness is fundamental to our ways of working. We've found that fiction processes provide powerful methodologies for practitioners engaged in all manner of work. We recognize the word 'humanness' as common ground.

Imagination. What has become clear during the research for this book is that the questions we ask as writers are shared by professionals in a range of other fields; the fiction approaches and techniques we rely on are not only important to other disciplines but already embedded within them. 'Real-life' disciplines are not gracious in bending an ear to what writers do but are often relying on our tools. It's just that sometimes they don't recognize what fiction might have to offer, and the shared processes need unearthing. Allowing imagination to take its place as a valid component of the research apparatus is a step towards bringing these methods to light.

These chapters have aimed to highlight the value of fiction writing as a uniquely flexible exploratory method. Through the harnessing of imaginative acts, fiction creates an inclusive and synthesizing intellectual territory, which naturally brings together creative practice, critical knowledge, physical encounter, sensory perception and emotional understanding. Alive to a range of different perspectives, fiction allows for the interconnections between idea and lived experience. The practice of fiction writing is a process grounded in complexity, ambiguity and inquiry. It is driven by the energy of the imagination. As such, it offers a dynamic gateway to interdisciplinary activity and allows inventive approaches to real-life problems. As creative arts subjects are increasingly under pressure to justify their significance and validity in contemporary education, work and life, this book makes a case for the importance and relevance of the imagination in all its forms, scientific and technical, spatial and literary, linguistic and visual – brought together in the writing of fiction.

Notes

Introduction

1   Roland Barthes, *Image, Music, Text*, trans Stephen Heath (London: Fontana Press, 1977), 79.

Chapter 1

1   Bruno Latour, *We Have Never Been Modern*, trans. C. Porter (Cambridge, MA: Harvard University Press, 1993), 73.

2   Bender (2007), 26 qtd, in *Writing Remains*, 6.

3   There is a useful discussion of this contested border between fact and fiction in Helden and Witcher (2020), qtd here 2, 5.

4   Strathern, M., 'Out of context: The persuasive fictions of anthropology', *Current Anthropology* 28 (1987): 251–81.

5   Van Helden (2020), 213.

6   Gill et al. (2022), 4.

7   Murray (1993), 183.

8   The conversations in this chapter all took place over video call. Taking into account the time differences among Australia, the United States and the UK added an immediate dimension to our discussions about the nature of time and its 'reality'.

9   Murray (1993), 24.

10 J. McGlade, quoted in Murray (1999), 141.

11 This quote is from Chapter 2, 'Flows of Clay', from an untitled MS in progress, which Professor Joyce was kind enough to share during my research for this book.

12 Pluciennik, M., 'Archaeological Narratives and Other Ways of Telling', *Current Anthropology*, 40 (1999): 653–678, 654.

13 Ibid., 656.

14 Ibid., 656.

15 Murray (1999), 158–9.

16 William Wordsworth, *The Prelude*, XII (1805), 206–19.

17 For the specific terms that help to unpick the complex layering proposed by Heidegger, see Paul Ricœur, 'Narrative Time', *Critical Inquiry*, Vol. 7, No. 1, (Autumn, 1980), 169–90.

18 Bakhtin, Mikhail M. 'Forms of Time and of the Chronotope in the Novel: Notes toward a Historical Poetics' in Holquist, Michael (ed.) *The Dialogic Imagination: Four Essays* (Austin, Texas: University of Texas Press, 1982), 84–5.

19 Morson and Emerson (1999), 374.

20 E. J. McCullough helpfully defines 'imaginative time' as a distinct way of experiencing time, alongside Functional, Foundational and Social time. See McCullough, E. J., *Time as a Human Resource* (Calgary: University of Calgary Press, 1992).

21 Alasdair MacIntyre, *After Virtue* 2nd ed. (South Bend: University of Notre Dame Press, 1984), 212.

22 Salman Rushdie, *Imaginary Homelands: Essays and Criticism 1981–1991* (London: Granta, 1992), 12.

23 Shane Barry, 'Silver Daggers and Russian Dolls: David Mitchell in Interview', *Three Monkeys Online*.

24 Jane Austen, *Persuasion*. Ed. by John Davie, (Oxford: Oxford World Classics. First published 1817. 1990), 223.

25 Ibid., p. 225.

26 M. M. Bakhtin, *The Dialogic Imagination: Four Essays* (Austin: University of Texas Press, 1981), 228.

27 E. L. Doctorow, *Homer and Langley* (London and New York: Random House, 2009), 14.

28 A good example of this can be seen by returning to *Tess of the d'Urbervilles,* in which Hardy grounds the ambitious sweep of the novel in evocative scenes that rely on detail and precision. So, when Tess's husband, Angel, lifts her from bed during a sleepwalking episode, and carries her out of the house wrapped in a sheet-shroud to lay her in an empty stone coffin, Hardy focuses the reader's attention on Angel 'slightly striking his stockinged toe against the edge of the door', on the missing handrail on the footbridge 'leaving the bare plank only', or the 'spots of froth' in the rapid river below. In so doing, time becomes conspicuous and clearly discernible. We are thrown into the scene in something approaching a real-life chronology, becoming acutely conscious of Angel lifting Tess and walking down the stairs from the

bedroom, of their passage along the dangerous riverside path and the walk through the Abbey to the empty tomb.

29 Gary Raymond, 'On the Black Hill', *Wales Arts Review* (26 January 2017).

30 Mark Ford, 'Thank God for John Rayburn', *London Review of Books* Vol. 13, No. 2. (24 January 1991).

31 Wilson (1942), 270.

32 Virginia Woolf, *The Diary of Virginia Woolf*, ed. Anne Olivier Bell, Vol. 2, (San Diego: Harcourt Brace, 1978), 263.

33 Joyce (2002), 1.

34 Ibid., 5, and also in conversation.

35 Gabriel Garcia Marquez, *Love in the Time of Cholera* (New York: Knopf, 1988), 293. It's interesting how often the word 'eternal' occurs in Márquez's novel, further highlighting issues of long and short time pertinent to the discussion in this chapter.

Chapter 2

1 Woolf (1924), 4, 6, 10.

2 This question has particular resonance with the development of AI and VR worlds, of course, but this discussion is beyond the scope of this chapter.

3 The remaining gaps (8 per cent) were completed with a full sequencing of the human genome by the Telomere-to-Telomere consortium in 2022. See, for example, Sergey Nurk, Sergey Koren et al., 'The complete sequence of a human genome', *Science* 2022, 376, 44–53.

4 There is some debate about the exact date when the term was first used, with claims for 1905, 1906 and 1909.

5 Raphael Falk, 'A century of Mendelism: on Johannsen's genotype conception', *International Journal of Epidemiology*, 2014, 43 (4), 1002–7.

6 Thomas Hunt Morgan, 'The Relation of Genetics to Physiology and Medicine', Nobel Lecture (4 June 1934), in *Nobel Lectures: Physiology or Medicine 1922–1941* (Amsterdam: Elsevier, 1965), 315.

7 Igor Zwir et al., 'Uncovering the complex genetics of human character', *Molecular Psychiatry* 2020, 25(10): 2295–312, 2295.

8 See, for example, Bratko D, Butković A, Vukasović T. 'Heritability of personality', *Psychological Topics*, 2017, 26 (1), 1–24.

9 David Funder, *The Personality Puzzle*, (New York: Norton, 2007), 1–2.

10 Plomin (2018), 83, 80.

11 Barker (2021), 5.

12 Ibid., 9.

13 Choksey (2021), 191.

14 Ibid.

15 A.S. Byatt, *On Histories and Stories* (London: Vintage, 2001), 166.

16 Vibhuti Patel. 'An Interview with Sir Salman Rushdie', *Wall Street Journal*, 27 November 2010.

17 Salman Rushdie, *The Satanic Verses* (London: Viking, 1988), 194.

18 Ibid., 168.

19 Ibid., 300.

20 Ibid., 284–5.

21 Ibid., 537–8.

22 Plomin (2018), 90.

23 Ian McEwan, 'Literature, Science and Human Nature', in Jonathan Gottschall and David Sloan Wilson (ed), *The Literary Animal. Evolution and the Nature of Narrative* (Evanston, Illinois: Northwestern University Press, 2005), 19.

24 Ian McEwan, *Saturday* (London: Vintage, 2006), 54.

25 Ibid., 189.

26 Ibid., 94.

27 Ibid., 94, 217.

28 David Amigoni, 'What is special about the gene? A literary perspective', *Genomics, Society and Policy* 2008, 4(1), 1–11, 10.

29 N. S. Wexler, 'Prejudice in a portrayal of Huntington's Disease', *The Lancet* 2005, 366 (9491), 1069–70, 1070.

30 McEwan (2006), 93.

31 Jane Austen, *Pride and Prejudice* ed. Vivien Jones (London: Penguin Classics, 2014), 58.

32 Mitchell (2023), 245.

33 See, for example, Bastiaan T. Heijmans, Elmar Tobi et al., 'Persistent epigenetic differences associated with pre-natal exposure to famine in humans', *Proceedings of the National Academy of Sciences* 2008, 105 (44), 17046–9.

34 Carey (2011), 235–6.

35. Ibid., 55.

36. For a useful overview of these arguments, see, for example, Maximilian Fitz-James, Giacomo Cavalli, 'Molecular mechanisms of transgenerational epigenetic inheritance', *Nature Reviews Genetics*, 2022, 23 (6), 325–41.

37. For a full discussion of transgenerational epigenetic inheritance see, for example, Jana Švorcová, 'Transgenerational epigenetic inheritance of traumatic experience in mammals', *Genes* January 2023, 14(1), 120, https://doi.org/10.3390/genes14010120

38. Kevin Mitchell, 'Epigenetics: What Impact does it have on our Psychology?', *The Conversation*, 24 January 2019.

39. Marianne Hirsch, *The Generation of Postmemory: Writing and Visual Culture after the Holocaust* (New York: Columbia University Press, 2012), 5.

40. Elif Shafak, *The Island of Missing Trees* (London: Penguin, 2022), 18.

41. Elif Shafak, *The Guardian*, 18 July 2021.

42. 'An Interview with Marianne Hirsch', *Author Interviews*, Columbia University Press, Author Interviews | Columbia University Press.

43. Samuel O'Donoghue, 'Postmemory as Trauma? Some Theoretical Problems and their Consequences for Contemporary Literary Criticism', *Politika* (2018), 5.

44. For further discussion, see Aleksandra Stelmach and Brigitte Nerlich, 'Metaphors in Search of a Target: The Curious Case of Epigenetics', *New Genetics and Society*, 2015, 34 (2), 196–218.

45. David Cox, 'How Genetics Determine our Life Choices', BBC Future 10 May 2023, https://www.bbc.com/future/article/20230509-how-genetics-determine-our-life-choices [accessed 11/01/24].

46. Michell (2023), 245.

47. Jerome de Groot, 'New Materialism, archaeogenetics and tracing the human' in Gill (2022), 35.

48. Ibid., 36.

49. Haruki Murakami, *Novelist as Vocation*, trans. Ted Goossen (New York: Knopf Publishing, 2022).

Chapter 3

1. Aravind Adiga, *Last Man in Tower* (London: Atlantic Books, 2012), 3.

2. Nor is this chapter concerned with 'fictional architecture', where the word 'fiction' is employed to highlight an act of imagination that allows architects to explore

possibilities with freedom: this is a term given to speculative architectural projects which will probably never be built, a method of testing alternative forms without the commitment or expense of construction work. While most writers will recognize elements of this free-flow speculation, my discussion here is concerned with the 'real' spaces of architecture, those contained within realized structures.

3   J. Kent Fitzsimons, 'The Double-Bind of Fictional Lives: Architecture and Writing in George Perec's *Life, A User's manual*' in Gadanho (2013), 159–68, 159.

4   Qtd in J. Oksanish, 'Vitruvius and the Programmatics of Prose', *Arethusa* 2016, 49(2), 263–280, 264.

5   Amy Butt, 'Endless forms, vistas and hues: Why architects should read science fiction', *Architectural Research Quarterly*, 22.2 (2018) 151–61, 154.

6   Conference notice, *Architecture News* (20 September 2010).

7   David Spurr, *Architecture and Modern Literature* (Ann Arbor: University of Michigan Press, 2012), 3.

8   John Hejduk, *Berlin Night* (Rotterdam: Nai Uitgevers, Netherlands Architecture Institute, 1993), 18.

9   Véronique Plesch, 'Literary Spaces' in Gadanho and Susana Oliveira (2013), 145–7, 145.

10 See, for example, Walter Benjamin, 'Paris: Capital of the Nineteenth Century', *Perspecta* 12 (1969), 163–72.

11 Coates (2012), 32, 161.

12 Robert Venturi, qtd. in Ken Allinson, 'Telling Tales', *Architectural Dialogue*, 1 April 2012.

13 Adrian Forty, *Words and Buildings: A Vocabulary of Modern Architecture* (London: Thames and Hudson, 2004) 120.

14 Ibid., 161.

15 Giuliana Bruno, *Atlas of Emotion: Journeys in Art, Architecture and Film* (London: Verso, 2002), 10–1.

16 Gadanho and Susana Oliveira (2013), 8.

17 Matteo Pericoli, (2018), 284.

18 Alice Munro, *Selected Stories* (Toronto: McClelland and Stewart, 1997), 1.

19 Michel de Certeau, *The Practice of Everyday Life*, (Berkeley: University of California Press, 1984), 115.

20 Ibid., 117.

21 Ibid.

22 Bakhtin (1982), 84–5.

23 Pericoli (2018), 288.

24 Matteo Pericoli, 'The Laboratory of Literary Architecture', online prospectus, lablitarch.com.

25 Pericoli (2018), 284.

26 Matteo Pericoli, 'Writers as Architects', *The New York Times*, 3 August 2013.

27 Orman Pamuk, 'Why didn't I become an architect?', in *Other Colours: Essays and a Story* (New York: Random House, 2007), 307.

28 Shohini Ghosh, 'Arundhati Roy: The City as Novel', Interview in *Aperture*, 2021, 243.

29 Rob Kitchen and James Kneale, 'Exploring imaginative geographies of the new millennium', *Progress in Human Geography* 25.1 (2001), 19–35, 19.

30 Dalila Colucci, Pier Luigi Sacco, 'A glint of lights in the fog: *Invisible Cities* and the riddles of planning practice', *Journal of Planning Education and Research* 2021, online, https://doi.org/10.1177/0739456X211027638 [accessed 12 June 2024].

31 Posthumously published interview in *The Paris Review*, qtd. in Vinit Mukhija, 'Learning from *Invisible Cities*: The interplay and dialogue of order and disorder', *Environment and Planning A: Economy and Space*, 2015 47 (4), 801–15, 808.

32 Borges uses the same word as the first letter of the Hebrew alphabet, which in Judaism signifies oneness and unity.

33 Jorge Luis Borges, *The Aleph and Other Stories 1933–1969*, trans. Norman Thomas di Giovanni, (London: Cape, 1971).

34 In his account of everyday life, de Certeau notes that seeing (Borges' repeated '*ver*') is largely a process of ordering, similar to the narrator's listing of the things he witnesses in *The Aleph*. By contrast, the spatial experience, de Certeau claims, is 'going', a process of movement, our everyday storytelling (as mundane as giving directions to a guest to find their way in our homes) predicated on the sense of a journey and the expectations of what this might result in. For the narrator in Borges' story, this journey is apparently made impossible not only by his being laid flat in a darkened cellar, but, later, by the physical destruction of the house on Garay Street. Nonetheless, he is clearly on a quest, looking in his continual return to the house for a way to lay to rest the pain of Beatriz's death, and in the postscript, struggling to understand the processes of memory and loss, absence and presence, who we are and what we experience.

35 Sylvan Barnet, William Burto, and William E. Cain (eds.), *An Introduction to Literature*, fourteenth edition (New York: Pearson, 2005), 400.

36 Pericoli (2018), 286.

37 Carola Hilfrich, qtd. Pericoli (2018), 300, 303.

Chapter 4

1. Kathryn Montgomery Hunter, *Doctors' Stories: The Narrative Structure of Medical Knowledge* (New Jersey: Princeton University Press, 1991), xvii, 149.
2. Femi Oyebode, *The Lancet*, Perspectives, vol. 402, 9 September 2023, 841.
3. Arisotle, *Poetics*, trans. Ingram Bywater, in *Introduction to Aristotle* ed. Richard McKeon (Chicago: University of Chicago Press, 1973), 678.
4. Paul Ricœur, 'Narrative Time' in *On Narrative*, ed. W. J. T. Mitchell (Chicago: University of Chicago Press, 1981), 167.
5. Brooks (1992), xiii.
6. E. M. Forster, *Aspects of the Novel* (London: Penguin, 1990), 89.
7. Brooks (1992), 4.
8. Ibid., 19.
9. Charon (2006), 49.
10. Ibid., vii.
11. Montgomery Hunter, 59–62.
12. David Morris, 'Narrative medicines: Challenge and resistance', *The Permanente Journal*, 12 (1) Winter 2008, 88–96, 91.
13. Ibid.
14. Charon, 50.
15. Ibid., 9-10. Charon considers a range of other writing techniques, including frame, form, time and desire, distinguishing the key narrative features of medicine as temporality, singularity, causality/contingency, intersubjectivity and ethicality. But for the purposes of this chapter, I am confining my attention to her discussion of plot.
16. Ibid., 124.
17. Ibid., 212.
18. Brooks (1992), 130.

Prior notes (continued from previous page):

38. Umberto Eco, 'The Art of Fiction No. 197', *The Paris Review*, 185, Summer 2008, https://www.theparisreview.org/interviews/5856/the-art-of-fiction-no-197-umberto-eco [accessed 23 October 2024].
39. 'About the Journal', *Interstices Journal of Architecture and Related Arts*, online edition, https://interstices.ac.nz/index.php/Interstices/about [accessed 23 October 2024].

19 Ibid., 64–5.

20 Montgomery Hunter, 139.

21 Ibid., 29.

22 Ibid., 31, 33.

23 John Launer, 'Conversations inviting change', *Postgraduate Medical Journal* 84 (957) February 2008, 4–5, my italics.

24 Peter Hühn et al., eds., *Handbook of Narratology* (Berlin: De Gruyter, 2009), 411. See also, for example, B. F. Sharf, M. L. Vanderford, 'Illness narratives and the social construction of health', in Dorsey A., Miller K. I., Parrott R., Thompson T., eds.*The Routledge Handbook of Health Communication* (New York: Routledge, 2003) and L. Kirmayer, A. Gomez-Carillo, 'Narrative Medicine', *Person Centered Medicine* (New York: Springer, 2023), 235–55.

25 For a useful analysis of the current state of narrative medicine, see Daniel A. Fox, Joshua M. Hauser, 'Exploring perception and usage of narrative medicine by physician speciality: A qualitive analysis', *Philosophy, Ethics and Humanities in Medicine*, 16 (7), 2021, https://doi.org/10.1186/s13010-021-00106-w [accessed 12 June 2024].

26 See, for example, David Morris, 'Narrative medicines: Challenge and resistance', *The Permanente Journal*, 12 (1) Winter 2008, 88–96.

27 Kim Krisberg, 'Narrative Medicine: Every Patient has a Story', *AAMC News*, 28 March 2017; Podcast: The Power of Narrative Medicine, *Canadian Medical Association Journal*, 9 January 2023 195 (1).

28 Launer (2018), 12.

Chapter 5

1 The French narratologist Gérard Genette identified focalization as separate from point of view in *Figures* (volume III, 1972). He considered the terms more or less synonymous, along with perspective, although later narratologists further separated them. For the purposes of this chapter, I will be addressing both point of view and focalization as expressions of the same storytelling technique.

2 Mikhail M. Bakhtin, *The Dialogic Imagination: Four Essays*. trans. Caryl Emerson and Micheal Holquist. (Austin: University of Texas Press, 1981), 319.

3 Dominick LaCapra, *Madame Bovary on Trial* (Ithaca, New York: Cornell University Press, 1982), 149.

4 Roy Pascal, *The Dual Voice: Free indirect speech and its functioning in the nineteenth-century European novel* (Manchester: Manchester University Press, 1977), 100.

5   Qtd. in LaCapra, 39. LaCapra's account of the novel's reception and trial is thorough and engaging.

6   Heffer (2018), 257; Larry Vogelman, defence lawyer, quoted in Pascual, 2015, 142.

7   Heffer (2018), 258.

8   Andrew Bricker, 'Is narrative essential to the law?: Precedent, case law and judicial emplotment', *Law, Culture and the Humanities* 15 (2), 2016, https://doi.org/10.1177/1743872115627413

9   For further details of Supardi's research see, for example, 'Language power in the courtroom: The use of persuasive features in the opening statement', *Indonesian Journal of Applied Linguistics* 6 (1), 2016, 70–8.

10 C. Heffer, *The Language of Jury Trial: A Corpus-Aided Analysis of Legal-Lay Discourse* (Basingstoke: Palgrave Macmillan, 2005), 75.

11 For further detail of historical cases, see Krisda Chaemsaithong, 'Interactive Patterns of the Opening Statement in criminal trials: A historical perspective', *Discourse Studies* 16 (3), 2014, 347–64. Examples quoted below are from the analysis provided in this work.

12 Georgia Wolfe, 'A Court Visit: Observing a criminal trial at the Old Bailey', *Chambers Student*, newsletter, 2017, https://chambersstudent.co.uk/wheretostart/newsletter/a-court-visit-observing-a-criminal-trial-at-the-old-bailey [accessed 9 August 2024].

13 Shehan Karunatilaka, *The Seven Moons of Maali Almeida* (London: Sort of Books, 2022), 384.

14 See Wolfe, 'A Court Visit: Observing a criminal trial at the Old Bailey', cited above.

15 See, for example, Nancy Pennington and Reid Hastie, 'Explaining the evidence: Tests of the story model for juror decision making', *Journal of Personality and Social Psychology*, 62 (2), 189–206.

16 BBC Radio 4, *Desert Island Discs*, 22 October 2010.

17 Jeanine Skorinko et al., 'Effects of perspective taking on courtroom decisions', *Journal of Applied Social Psychology*, 44 (4), 2014, 303–18.

18 Ibid., 314

19 Roy Pascal, *The Dual Voice: Free indirect speech and its functioning in the nineteenth-century European novel* (Manchester: Manchester University Press, 1977), 9.

20 This subtle shuffle of point of view becomes particularly complex in the case of those prosecuting murder cases, where the victim cannot act as witness or speak for themselves. Throughout such a trial, the prosecuting counsel is compelled to fully voice another person, necessarily manifesting the emotional, and physical, reality experienced by the victim.

21 Qtd. in Brooks (1996), 168.

22 Heffer (2016), 267–8.

23 Stygall (2012), 373.

24 Toni Morrison, *Beloved* (London: Picador, 1988), 3.

25 Ibid., 7.

26 Ibid., 149. A word now recognized as offensive has been removed from this quotation.

27 Statement of ICC Prosecutor, Karim A. A. Khan QC, At The Opening of The Trial In The Case of The Prosecutor V. Ali Muhammad Ali Abd-Al-Rahman, International Criminal Court, 'News', 6 April 2022. [accessed on 15 April 2024].

28 *Beloved.*, 220.

29 'A Court Visit: Observing a criminal trial at the Old Bailey', *Chambers Student*, newsletter, 2017.

30 Ibid.

31 Ibid.

32 Anita K. Barry, 'Constructing a narrative in courtroom testimony', *Michigan Bar Journal*, July 1992, 830–833, 833.

33 Bader Nasser Aldosari, 'Questioning strategies in courtrooms', *World Journal of English Language*, 14 (2), 2024, 376.

34 Ibid., 382. Further examples and analysis of such strategies can be examined in Aldosari's article.

35 Ibid., 384.

36 Mohsin Zaidi, *A Dutiful Boy: A memoir of a gay Muslim boy's journey to acceptance* (London: Square Peg, 2020), 274.

37 Rhian Sasseen, 'Writing Is a Monstrous Act: A Conversation with Hernan Diaz', *Paris Review*, 2 June 2022.

Chapter 6

1 John Ruskin, *Modern Painters* IV (London: George Allen, 1860), 311.

2 It should also be noted that table-top games, film, comics and video and simulation games all rely to a greater or lesser extent on similar worldbuilding skills, but for the purposes of this discussion, the focus here will be on what we do as fiction writers.

3 Gagliano (2017), x.

4 John Ruskin, *Modern Painters* III (London: George Allen, 1860), 11.

5   See, for example, *The Power of Movement of Plants* (1880) written by Charles Darwin and his son, Francis, to highlight the revolutionary idea of a sensitive brain-like organ in a plant's embryonic root.

6   Emanuele Coccia, 'Francis Hallé: A Life Drawing Trees', *L'Officiel*, December 2019.

7   Arundhati Roy, *The God of Small Things* (London: Penguin, 1997), 124.

8   Qtd. Glotfelty (2012), 2.

9   Meeker (2019), 174.

10 Bishop (2020), 4–5.

11 Meeker (2019), 16.

12 Ibid., 16, 177–8.

13 Pat Murphy, 'His Vegetable Wife', in Ursula K. Le Guin and Brian Attebery (eds), *The Norton Book of Science Fiction* (New York: Norton, 1993), 628–32, 628.

14 Ibid., 632.

15 See, for example, Alpi, A. et al., 'Plant neurobiology: No brain, no gain?' *Trends in Plant Science* (2007) 12, 135–136.

16 See, for example, Michael Pollan, 'The Intelligent Plant: Scientists debate a new way of understanding flora', *The New Yorker*, 23 and 30 December (2013), 94.

17 Mancuso (2015), 4–5.

18 Michael Marder, 'Of plants and other secrets', *Societies*, 3, 2013, 16–23, 17.

19 Michael Marder, 'A philosophy of stories plants tell', *Narrative Culture*, 10 (2), 2023, 189–205, 189.

20 Ibid., 193.

21 See, for example, Frederike Middelhoff and Arnika Peselmann, 'The stories plants tell: An introduction to vegetal narrative cultures', *Narrative Culture*, 10 (2), 2023, 175–188.

22 Michael Marder, 'A philosophy of stories plants tell', *Narrative Culture*, 10 (2), 2023, 189–205, 196.

23 Ibid.

24 Ibid., 202.

25 John Wyndham, *The Day of the Triffids* (London: Penguin Classics, 2001), 22–3.

Three Words

1 Madeleine L'Engle, *A Wrinkle in Time* (London: Puffin, 2018), 45.

2 Roland Barthes, *The Pleasure of the Text* (New York: Farrar, Straus & Giroux, 1975), 18.

3 Colin Fournier, 'Urban Fictions', in Gadanho and Oliviera (2013), 19.

Selected Bibliography

Allison, John M., 'Narrative and time: A phenomenological reconsideration', *Text and Performance Quarterly*, 1994, 14, 108–25

Barker, Clare, 'Global genetic fictions', *Medical Humanities*, June 2021, 47 (2), 129–34

Belzer, Keith, 'Theater and film techniques, persuasion and courtroom choreography', *The Champion*, December 2019, 34–40

Bender, B., S. Hamilton, C. Tilley, E. Anderson, *Stone Worlds: Narrative and Reflexivity in Landscape Archaeology* (Walnut Creek: Left Coast Press, 2007)

Bishop, Katherine E., David Higgins and Jerry Määtä (eds), *Plants in Science Fiction: Speculative Vegetation* (Cardiff: University of Wales Press, 2020)

Bloomfield, Mandy and Clare Hanson, 'Beyond the gene: Epigenetic science in twenty-first century culture', *Textual Practice*, 2015, 29 (3), 405–13

Brooks, Peter, *Reading for the Plot: Design and Intention in Narrative* (Cambridge, Mass.: Harvard University Press, 1992)

Brooks, Peter and Paul Gewitz (eds), *Law's Stories: Narrative and Rhetoric in the Law* (New Haven and London: Yale University Press, 1996)

Carey, Nessa, *The Epigenetics Revolution: How Modern Biology is Rewriting Our Understanding of Genetics, Disease and Inheritance* (London: Icon Books, 2011)

Carr, David, *Time, Narrative and History* (Bloomington/Indianapolis: Indiana University Press, 1986)

Charon, Rita, *Narrative Medicine: Honoring the Stories of Illness* (Oxford: Oxford University Press, 2006)

Charon, Rita, Sayantani DasGupta, Nellie Hermann, Craig Irvine, Eric R. Marcus, et al., *The Principles and Practice of Narrative Medicine* (Oxford: Oxford University Press, 2016)

Choksey, Lara, *Narrative in the Age of the Genome* (London: Bloomsbury Academic, 2021)

Coates, Nigel, *Narrative Architecture* (London: Wiley, 2012)

Coles, Robert, *The Call of Stories: Teaching and the Moral Imagination* (Houghton Miffin: Boston, 1989)

Dyke, R. van, and R. Bernbeck, *Subjects and Narratives in Archaeology* (Denver: University Press of Colorado, 2015)

Gadanho, P., and Oliveira, S. (eds), *Once Upon a Place: Architecture and Fiction* (Lisbon: Caleidoscópio, 2013)

Gagliano, M., Ryan, J. C. and Vieira, P. *The Language of Plants: Science, Philosophy, Literature* (Minneapolis: University of Minnesota Press, 2017)

Gill, Josie, *Biofictions: Race, Genetics and the Contemporary Novel* (London: Bloomsbury, 2020)

Gill, J., C. J. McKenzie, E. Lightfoot (eds), *Writing Remains: New Intersections of Archaeology, Literature and Science* (London: Bloomsbury, 2022)

Gottschall, J., D. Wilson (eds), *The Literary Animal. Evolution and the Nature of Narrative* (Evanston, Illinois: Northwestern University Press, 2005)

Glotfelty, Cheryll, K. Armbruster, T. Lynch (eds), *The Bioregional Imagination: Literature, Ecology and Place* (London and Athens: University of Georgia Press, 2012)

Gracia, Diego, 'On Clinical History', Isabel Fernandez et al., *Creative Dialogues: Narrative and Medicine* (Cambridge: Cambridge Scholars Publishing, 2015)

Hamner, Everett, *Editing the Soul: Science and Fiction in the Genome Age* (Pennsylvania: Pennsylvania State University Press, 2017)

Hanson, Clare, *Genetics and the Literary Imagination* (Oxford: Oxford University Press, 2020)

Heffer, Chris, 'Narrative Practices and Voice in Court', *Handbook of Communication in the Legal Sphere* ed. Jacqueline Visconti (Berlin: De Gruyter, 2018), 256–87

Helden, D. van, R. Witcher (eds), *Researching the Archaeological Past through Imagined Narratives: A Necessary Fiction* (Abingdon and New York: Routledge, 2020)

Hunter, Kathryn Montgomery, *Doctors' Stories* (New Jersey: Princeton University Press, 1991)

Joyce, Rosemary, *The Languages of Archaeology: Dialogue, Narrative and Writing* (London: Blackwell, 2002)

Keller, Evelyn Fox, *The Century of the Gene* (Cambridge, Mass.: Harvard University Press, 2000)

Launer, John, *Narrative-based Practice in Health and Social Care. Conversations Inviting Change* (London: Routledge, 2018)

Mancuso, Stefano and Alessandra Viola, *Brilliant Green. The Surprising History and Science of Plant Intelligence* (Washington: Island Press, 2015)

Marder, Michael, *The Philosopher's Plant: An Intellectual Herbarium* (New York: Columbia University Press, 2014

McCullough, E.J., *Time as a Human Resource* (Calgary: University of Calgary Press, 1992)

Meeker, Natania and Antonia Szabari, *Radical Botany: Plants and Speculative Fiction* (New York: Fordham University Press, 2019)

Mitchell, Kevin, *Innate: How the Wiring of Our Brain Shapes Who We Are* (New Jersey: Princeton University Press, 2020)

Mitchell, Kevin, *Free Agents: How Evolution Gave Us Free Will* (New Jersey: Princeton University Press, 2023)

Morson, Gary, Emerson, Caryl, *Mikhail Bakhtin, Creation of a Prosaics* (Stanford: Stanford University Press, 1999)

Murray, Tim, 'Archaeology and the threat of the past: Sir Henry Rider Haggard and the acquisition of time', *World Archaeology*, 1993, 25 (2), 175–86

Murray, Tim, *Time and Archaeology* (London; New York: Routledge, 1999)

Pascual, Esther, *Fictive Interaction: The Conversation Frame in Thought, Language and Discourse* (Amsterdam: John Benjamins, 2015)

Pericoli, Mateo, 'The Laboratory of Literary Architecture', *The Routledge Companion on Architecture, Literature and the City* ed. Jonathan Charley (London: Routledge, 2018), 283–305

Plomin, Robert, *Blueprint: How DNA Makes Us Who We Are* (London: Allen Lane, 2018)

Richardson, Brian, ed., *Narrative Dynamics: Essays on Time, Plot, Closure and Frames* (Columbus: Ohio State University Press, 2002)

Ricœur, Paul, trans. McLaughlin and Pellauer, *Time and Narrative* (Chicago: University of Chicago Press, 1984)

Rose, Stephen, Leon Kamin, R. C. Lewontin, *Not in Our Genes: Biology, Ideology and Human Nature* (London: Penguin, 1984)

Stygall, Gail, 'Discourse in the US Courtroom', *The Oxford Handbook of Language and Law* (Oxford: Oxford University Press, 2012), 369–80

Wilson, James Southall, 'Time and Virginia Woolf', *The Virginia Quarterly Review*, 1942, 18 (2), 267–76

Zwir, I., Arnedo, J., Del-Val, C. et al. 'Uncovering the complex genetics of human character', *Molecular Psychiatry,* 2020, 25, 2295–312

Index

Aldosari, B. N. 126-7
The Aleph (Borges) 75-8
Amigoni, D. 48
Angrist, M., conversation with 41-43, 48-9, 59-60
archaeology
    Armit, I., conversation with 24-5, 26-7
    author's experience on dig 9-10
    chronologies, understanding of 16
    'deep time,' expressing 13-15
    dramatization, importance of 31
    engagement with narrative and story 3
    fictional accounts of events/sites 13
    humanness of time 31
    instants/long periods of time 24-5
    Joyce, R., conversation with 17, 18-19, 30-2, 33
    meta narratives of 25-6
    of multiplicity and simultaneity 17-19
    Murray, T., conversation with 14-16, 18-19
    narrative, use of in 12
    narrative time, recognition and manipulation of 19
    novels, archaeological sites and 32
    objects as texts 11-12
    past and present, aligning/differentiating 15
    scenes, excavations as 26
    speculative summaries in excavation reports 27-8
    'structure' and 'event,' interaction between 14, 15
    time in 10
    unreliable narrators, archaeologists as 31
    writing about, evolution of 11
architecture
    animating and imagining space, fiction as 80
    background/interest in, writers' 74
    Beyond project 67
    buildings/books, correspondences between 65-7
    challenges faced 72-3
    as characters in fiction 62
    engagement with narrative and story 3-4
    fictional spaces 69
    fiction as expressing ideas about 67-8
    Gadanho, P., conversation with 67-8, 69, 80
    Grice, G., conversation with 65, 80
    as infusing fiction 78-79
    Laboratory of Literary Architecture 72
    meaning of 66
    narrative architecture 64-5
    Pericoli, M., conversation with 71-3, 79-80
    reading/readers 72
    re-imagining and repurposing of spaces 69
    shared project with fiction 62-3
    skin and underlying space, writing as 73
    space 66-7
    space, fiction and 68-73, 75-8
    spatial, stories as 70

theme parks, story as embedded in 65
urban settings in fiction 74–5
visualization, skill of, fiction and 80
and writing/literature 63–65
Aristotle 85, 87
Armit, I., conversation with 24–5, 26–7
artificial intelligence (AI) 86
Austen, J. 23, 24, 26
authenticity of characters 36

Bachelard, G. 67
Bakhtin, M. 20, 24, 70–1, 107
Barchester Towers (Trollope) 106–7
Barker, C. 44
Barry, A. 126
Barthes, R. 4, 152
behavioural traits 40
Being and Time (Heidegger) 19
believability of characters 36
Beloved (Morrison) 121–124
Belzer, K. 115–116, 120, 128, 129
Bender, B. 12
Benjamin, W. 65
Beyond project 67
Bishop, K. 139
Bleak House (Dickens) 87
The Body Snatchers (film) 133–4
Booker, C. 85
books/buildings, correspondences between 65–6, 67
Borges, J. L. 75–8
botanical science
    Cade, O., conversation with 139–142
    commonality 139–140
    common/outlandish juxtaposition 140
    complexity of plants, storytelling and 147–8
    creative imagination, importance of 138–9
    fiction as informing 149–50
    imaginative act, value of 137
    large/small interaction 131–2, 135–7, 147
    literature, plants in 133–4
    milieu 148
    plants, domination of in environment 132
    questions, fiction as raising 150
    Rao, N., conversation with 135–7, 144
    sentience/intelligence of plants 141–7
    Sloan, J., conversation with 146–7, 148–50, 151
    speculative fiction and 139–144
    unfamiliar other, plants as 134–5
    wonder, sense of 141
    worldbuilding and 133, 148–9
Bricker, A. 110
Brilliant Green: The Surprising History and Science of Plant Intelligence (Mancuso and Viola) 145–6
Brooks, P. 87, 95
Bruno, G. 67
Buddenbrooks (Mann) 25
Buell, L. 138
buildings/books, correspondences between 65–6, 67
Byatt, A.S. 45

Cade, O., conversation with 139–41, 144
Calvino, I. 74–5
Carey, N. 54–5
case histories. *see* medicine
characters
    Angrist, M., conversation with 41–43, 45, 48–9, 60
    believability of 36
    changes in, genetics and 41–42, 53–8
    conflicts and choices, continued importance of 59
    creating, genetics and 47–9
    epigenetics 53–8
    fiction's contribution to genetics 59–60
    Gattaca (film) 42
    importance of in fiction 35–6
    language barrier 60
    Mitchell, K., conversation with 50–1, 55, 58
    modern age, creating in 36–7
    as multitemporal 58–9

Nerlich, B., conversation with 55–6, 58, 60
  personality 40
  small differences, importance of 50
  temperament 40
  transactional characterisation 44–5
Charon, R. 88–9, 91, 93–4
Chatwin, B. 27
childhood trauma, changes in genes and 54
Choksey, L. 44
chronologies, understanding of in archaeology 16
chronotopes 20, 70–1
cities in fiction 74–5
Clare, J. 133
close third-person point of view 106–8
Cloud Atlas (Mitchell) 23
Coates, N. 65, 66
Conversations Inviting Change 101–2
courtrooms, trials in. *see* criminal trials
creative writing techniques, choice of 6–7
criminal trials
  explicit manipulation of point of view 115–17
  first-person narration 112–13
  fragmentation of discourse 111
  impact of point of view 129
  lack of attention given to fiction techniques 129
  narrative, trials as form of 129
  narrative and plot in 109
  opening statements 111–13
  point of view and 108–9
  questions, use of in 125–7
  second-person point of view in 113–18
  Skorinko, J., conversation with 116–18
  story, sense of 109–10
  storytelling techniques and 110
  Supardi, S., conversation with 110, 111, 112, 129
  third-person point of view 118–21
  trust and truth, point of view and 128–9
  'we' point of view 113

Dahl, R. 150
Dante 133
The Day of the Triffids (Wyndham) 149
de Certeau, M. 70
'deep time'
  archaeology and 13–15
  fiction, expressing in 28
de Groot, J. 59
Díaz, H. 128
Dickens, C. 87, 95–6, 101
DNA. *see* genetics
Doctorow, E. L. 26
Droysen, J. 2
A Dutiful Boy (Zaidi) 128

Eco, U. 78–81
Eliot, G. 77
The Environmental Imagination (Buell) 138
epigenetics 53–8
'event' and structure', interaction between 14, 15
excavation reports, speculative summaries in 26–7

fiction
  focus on 5
  multiplicity and simultaneity of time 17–18
first-person narration in criminal trials 112–3
Fitzsimons, J. K. 62, 68
Flaubert, G. 107–8
The Flowering of the Strange Orchid (Wells) 133
Flynn, G. 105–6
Ford, M. 27
Forster, E. M. 87
Forty, A. 66
Fournier, C. 152–3
free indirect discourse 106–8
Funder, D. 40

Gadanho, P., conversation with 67–8, 69, 80
garden metaphor for plot 83–4

genetics
    Angrist, M., conversation with 41–44, 45, 48–9, 59–60
    changes in characters and 40–1, 44–5, 53–8
    character and 41
    conflicts and choices, continued importance of 59
    creating a character and 47–9
    epigenetics 53–8
    fiction's contribution to 59–60
    focus of research in 38
    Gattaca (film) 42
    'gene,' emergence of term 38–9
    gene regulation 53
    genes, changes to 52–8
    humanity, fiction as intrinsic to, Rushdie on 45–7
    increased knowledge about 37
    as limited to speculative genres 42
    Mitchell, K., conversation with 50–1, 55, 58
    Nerlich, B., conversation with 55–6, 57–8, 60
    personality 40
    postmemory 56–7
    questions raised by 39
    real life issues in fiction 43–4
    speed of change, fiction and 45
    temperament 40
    threat and doom in fiction 43
    traits 40
    transactional characterisation 44–5
The God of Small Things (Roy) 136
Gone Girl (Flynn) 105–6
Great Expectation (Dickens) 94–5
Grice, G., conversation with 65, 80

Hardy, T. 26, 74
Hastings, S., conversation with 95–8, 102, 104
Heffer, C. 109–10, 119
Heidegger, M. 19
Hermann, N., conversation with 91–3
Hilfrich, C. 80

Hirsch, M. 57
Homer and Langley (Doctorow) 26
Human Genome Project 37
humanities/sciences, split between 2–3
humanness
    curiosity about 152–3
    of time 31
Hunter, K. M. 84, 89, 98, 99

identity, time and 30
imagination
    application of 2–3
    'real-life' disciplines' use of 153
The Inferno (Dante) 133
inherited pain 57
intelligence, plant 142–6
internet, patients' use of 90
Invasion of the Body Snatchers (film) 134
Invisible Cities (Calvino) 74–5
The Island of Missing Trees (Shafak) 57

Johannsen, W. 38
Joyce, R., conversation with 17, 18, 31, 33

Karunatilaka, S. 113
Kincaid, J. 134

Laboratory of Literary Architecture 72
language and object, link between 11
Latour, B. 10
Launer, J., conversation with, 1002, 103–4
law
    engagement with narrative and story 3
    explicit manipulation of point of view 115–8
    first-person narration in trials 112–13
    fragmentation of discourse 111
    impact of point of view 129
    lack of attention given to fiction techniques 129
    narrative, trials as form of 129
    narrative and plot in 109
    opening statements in trials 111–13

point of view and 118–9
questions, use of in trials 125–7
second-person point of view in trials 113–18
Skorinko, J., conversation with 116–18
story, sense of 109–110
storytelling techniques and 110
Supardi, S., conversation with 110, 111, 112, 129
third-person point of view in criminal trials 118–121
trust and truth, point of view and 128–9
'we' point of view in trials 113
L'Engle, M. 152
limited/close third-person point of view 106–8
'lines of desire,' 61
linguistics, archaeology and 11
listening skills 93
literary analysis, archaeology and 11

McEwan, I. 47
McGlade, J. 16
MacIntyre, A. 21
Madame Bovary (Flaubert) 107–8
Mancuso, S. 145–6
Mann, T. 25
Mansfield, M. 115
Marder, M. 146, 148
Márquez, G. G. 33
medicine
  caution re. plotting in real life 103–4
  closure of patient's story 99
  Conversations Inviting Change 101–2
  Hastings, S., conversation with 95–8, 102, 104
  Hermann, N., conversation with 91–3
  imagination and creativity, using in 91–2
  internet, patients' use of 90
  Launer, J., conversation with 103–47
  listening skills 93
  medical histories 89–91, 96–8
  medical histories, plot and 93–4

  muddle of life 95–6
  narrative 84–5, 88, 89–90, 102–3
  participatory plotting 100–1
  plot and 85
  psychiatric, pitfalls of applying plot to 97
  reading, importance of 92
  re-ordering plots 102
  rewriting patients' stories by doctors 99
  therapeutic dialogue 101
  time, medical histories and 97–8
  unnarrative 95–6
  unpredictability of personal narratives 90–3
Meeker, N. 138, 140
memory, fiction and 21–2
meta narratives of archaeology 25–6
Middlemarch (Eliot) 77
milieu 148
Mitchell, D. 22
Mitchell, K., conversation with 50–1, 55, 58
Modernist architecture and writing 63
Morgan, T. H. 38
Morrison, T. 121–3
motifs in novels 19–20
Mr. Bennett and Mrs. Brown (Woolf) 36
multitemporal, characters as 58–9
Munro, A. 69, 72, 79
Murakami, H. 59
Murray, T., conversation with 14–16, 18, 29
mutuality 5
My Garden (Book) (Kincaid) 134

The Name of the Rose (Eco) 78–9, 79–81
narrative architecture 64–5
narrative medicine 84–5, 88, 89–90, 102–3
narratives
  memories and life stories 3
  use of term 6
narrative structure. *see* architecture
narrative theory, approach to 5–6
narrative time
  in fiction 18–26

recognition and manipulation of in archaeology 18
Nerlich, B., conversation with 55–6, 57–8, 60

objects
　and language, link between 11
　as texts 11–12
On the Black Hill (Chatwin) 27
opening statements in criminal trials 111–13
opposition to story and narrative 4
Oyebode, F. 85

Pamuk, O. 74
participatory plotting 100–1
Pascal, R. 108, 119
past and present, archaeology and 15
Pericoli, M., conversation with 71–3, 79–80
personality 40
perspective
　Beloved (Morrison) 121–23
　manipulation of in criminal trials 115–18
　uncertainty due to manipulation of 121–23
　see also point of view in criminal trials
Persuasion (Austen) 23, 24, 26
place, evocation of. *see* worldbuilding
plants
　blindness to 132
　Cade, O., conversation with 139–42
　commonality, –139–40
　common/outlandish juxtaposition 140
　complexity of, storytelling and 147–8
　creative imagination, importance of 138–9
　domination of in environment 132
　fiction as informing science of 149–50
　imaginative act, value of 137
　large/small interaction 135–7, 147
　in literature 133–4
　milieu 148

　questions, fiction as raising 150
　Rao, N., conversation with 135–7, 144
　sentience/intelligence of 141–7
　Sloan, J., conversation with 146, 148–50, 151
　speculative fiction and 139–144
　as unfamiliar other 134–5
　wonder, sense of 141
　worldbuilding and 133, 148–9
Plesch, V. 65
Plomin, R. 40, 146–7
plot
　caution re. plotting in real life 103–4
　closure of patient's story 99
　Conversations Inviting Change 101–2
　in fiction 85–6
　garden metaphor for 83–4
　internet, patients' use of 90
　listening skills 93
　medical histories 89–90, 92–4, 96–8
　medicine and 85
　misunderstanding of hidden 95
　muddle of life 95–6
　multiple temporalities in 86–7
　narrative medicine 85–6, 88, 89–90
　participatory plotting 100–1
　pattern, imposition of 86
　psychiatric medicine, pitfalls of applying to 96–7
　reader's role and 87–8
　re-ordering 102
　rewriting patients' stories by doctors 99
　serial publications 94–5
　as significant technique in fiction 88
　therapeutic dialogue 101
　time, connection with 86
　time, medical histories and 97–8
　unfolding of hidden purpose 86
　unpredictability of personal narratives 90–1
　use of term 6
　value of in medicine 103–4
Pluciennik, M. 17–18
point of view in criminal trials

Beloved (Morrison) 121–3
   explicit manipulation of 115–8
   first-person narration 112–3
   fragmentation of discourse 109
   free indirect discourse 106–108
   impact of 129
   lack of attention given to 129
   limited/close third-person 106–8
   multiple perspectives in trials 108–9
   narrative, trials as form of 129
   opening statements 111–13
   persuasion 110–11
   questions, use of 125–7
   rabbit-duck illusion 105
   second-person 113–18
   switching between different 105–6
   third-person 118–21
   trust and truth 128–9
   uncertainty due to manipulation of 121–4
   'we' form 113
Pollan, M. 145
postmemory 56–7
The Prelude (Wordsworth) 19
psychiatry 95–7

questions
   botanical science, fiction as raising 150
   criminal trials, use of in 125–8
   genetics 39

Raban, J. 27
rabbit-duck illusion 105
Radical Botany (Meeker and Szabari) 138, 140
Rao, N., conversation with 135–8, 144
reading between the lines 61
reading/readers
   architecture 72
   landscapes and objects 11
   medical histories 92–3
   plot and 87–8
   role of the reader 151–3

Richard II (Shakespeare) 133
Ricœur, P. 85
Roy, A. 74, 136
Rushdie, S. 22, 45–7, 54
Ruskin, J. 131, 133

The Satanic Verses (Rushdie) 45–8, 54
Saturday (McEwan) 47
Scarry, E. 119
scenes, excavations as 26
sciences/humanities, split between 2–3
scientific methods 2
second-person point of view in criminal trials 113–18
sense of self and identity, time and 30
sentience of plants 141–7
serial publications 94–5
The Seven Moons of Maali Almeida (Karunatilaka) 113
Shafak, E. 57
Shakespeare, W. 133
Skorinko, J., conversation with 116–18
Sloan, J., conversation with 146–8, 148–50, 151
'The Sound Machine' (Dahl) 150
space
   architecture and 66–7
   fiction and 68–73, 75–8
speculative fiction, plants and 139–44
speculative summaries in excavation reports 26–7
spots of time, influence of 19
Spurr, D. 64
Stefánsson, K 58
story
   memories and life stories 3
   use of term 6
Structuralism 11
'structure' and 'event,' interaction between 14, 15
Stygall, G. 120
Supardi, S., conversation with 110, 111, 112, 129
Szabari, A. 138, 140

temperament 40
Tess of the D'Urbervilles (Hardy) 26
theme parks, story as embedded in 65
third-person point of view in criminal trials 118–21
Thompson, V. 13
time
  in archaeology 10
  author's experience on archaeological dig 9–10
  chronologies, understanding of in archaeology 16
  chronotopes 20
  'deep time', expressing 14
  as elastic and personal 29
  in fiction 13, 15–16, 19–26
  as fluid and unpredictable in fiction 22
  humanness of 31
  instants/long periods 23–5
  juggling of past and present 20–1
  medical histories and 97–8
  motifs in novels 19–20
  multiple layers, experience of 19
  multiplicity and simultaneity of 16–18
  narrative, in archaeology 18
  past and present, archaeology and 15
  plot, connection with 86
  sense of self and identity 30
  spots of time, influence of 19
  story and discourse methodology for fiction 20
traits 40
transactional characterization 44–5
transgenerational inheritance 54–55

trauma in childhood, changes in genes and 54
trials, criminal. *see* criminal trials

unfamiliar other, plants as 134–5
unnarrative medicine 95–6
unreliable narrators
  archaeologists as 31–2
  patients/criminal defendants as 119
urban settings in fiction 74–5

'The Vegetable Wife' (Murphy) 142–144
Venturi, R. 66
Viola, A. 145–6
Vitruvius 63
Voruganti, I. 103

Wells, H. G. 131
'we' point of view in trials 111
Wexler, N. 46
wonder, sense of, plants and 139
Woolf, V. 28–30, 36
Wordsworth, W. 19
worldbuilding
  botanical science and 131
  imaginative act, value of 135
  large/small interaction 129–32, 133–5
  milieu, plants and 146
writing, engaging with landscapes and objects 11
Wyndham, J. 147

Zaidi, M. 126